Unique NEWS

Naresh Chandra Mathur

PUSTAK MAHAL®

Administrative office and sale centre

J-3/16 , Daryaganj, New Delhi-110002
☎ 23276539, 23272783, 23272784 • *Fax:* 011-23260518
E-mail: info@pustakmahal.com • *Website:* www.pustakmahal.com

Branches
Bengaluru: ☎ 080-22234025 • *Telefax:* 080-22240209
E-mail: pustak@airtelmail.in • pustak@sancharnet.in
Mumbai: ☎ 022-22010941, 022-22053387
E-mail: rapidex@bom5.vsnl.net.in
Patna: ☎ 0612-3294193 • *Telefax:* 0612-2302719
E-mail: rapidexptn@rediffmail.com

ISBN 978-81-223-1500-4

Edition: 2014

Printed at : Ar Emm International, New Delhi

Preface

After my retirement as a banker, I was unsure of my future plans. But I knew life offers plenty of opportunities to every individual to fulfil the dreams and pursue the happiness. Man in his journey from the womb to the tomb, has one wish - to be happy. My present work is a small step towards achieving this goal for myself and for my readers. To be stress-free and relaxed, even for some moments in life is the aim of this book - a compilation of **"Unique News"** from local newspapers of recent past. This collection is sure to energise your nerves, brighten up your face and lighten your mind. Usually we read a book from start to finish for the purpose of connectivity. This adds to some stress in reading. But **"Unique News"** can be read comfortably in a piecemeal and every piece transport you instantly to another world. You can enjoy reading this book with your friends as well and create some light moments.

The book is dedicated to my family, relatives, friends and all those who inspired the instinct of an author in me. I am immensely grateful to each one of them. Life is such that worries, sadness and dismay can overtake you any time. It is solely up to the individual to keep those feelings at bay and attract happiness, yes, and instant happiness. You decide to be happy and you are happy! So, here's a book to make you SMILE which is below your nose. Meanwhile, I regret for everything.

With ***'Namastey Mathur'***

Naresh Chandra Mathur
Anupama Apartment, Flat No.2-A
Nala Road, Behind Petrol Pump
PATNA-800004 (Bihar)
Email: nareshchandramathur@gmail.com
M#: 09955115542 & **LL:** 0612-2721604

The Pursuit of Happiness

At a time when no news seems to be good news, I compiled **UNIQUE News** of newspapers to dispel the gloom and doom, and celebrate the joys of life (***Khud Khushi***).

श्रम एव जयते

DASHRATH MANJHI – 'THE MOUNTAIN MAN'

Gaya: It is an amazing story of a poor man called Dashrath Manjhi who carved out a mountain to create a path for the sake of his wife, Falguni Devi. Manjhi had worked single-handedly for 22 years, from 1960 to 1982, to carve a 360 feet long road, 25 feet deep & 30 feet wide across the Gehlour hills in Gaya, some 100 km. south-east of Patna with a hammer, chisel and nails. Manjhi embarked on the project after his wife died, wondering why one had to take a circuitous 70 km. route around a mountain to get medical help when the distance was a mere 5-6 km. as the crow flies. The Bihar government had felicitated him for his stellar act. He died on 17th August,

2007. He was suffering from cancer of gall bladder. The Bihar government accorded him a state funeral. Bollywood director Ketan Mehta, who has successfully completed his film "Manjhi – The Mountain Man". Folklore has it that after completing the road, Manjhi "walked for two months to reach New Delhi but could not fulfill his desire to meet the President of India."

Film Actor Aamir Khan visited the Manjhi Memorial to ***pay homage to the poor man's "Shah Jahan".*** Aamir who was truly inspired and moved by Manjhi's achievement, said, Manjhi has shown that nothing is impossible. His history is one of conviction and courage. Khan has ended the first season of ***Satyamev Jayate II*** with a mention of Manjhi's inspirational story.

It is important to know that words don't move mountains. ***Work,*** *exacting* ***work*** *moves mountains.*

Whenever you are overwhelmed by something, either you cry or you laugh. Crying is not necessarily sad, laughter is not necessarily joyous. Sometimes crying is a joy, sometimes laughter is ugly and may be just a device to hide your sadness.

Fasten your seat belts and let us embark on a roller coaster ride of some of the most fascinating and interesting bits of news from our vast country.

1. This buffalo is a 'khaini' addict

Lohardaga: **"Khaini (raw tobacco)"** is quite popular in this part of the country. Khaini addicts just put it under their lips and get the divine kick which nothing else can give them, This habit has taken every part of the society – rich or poor, young or old – by storm. Interestingly, it has now "infected" the bovine world also. Meet Mangra Munda's buffalo! It has become addicted to chewing tobacco, much to the surprise and discomfiture of its master. It demands six ample doses of "khaini" every day, without fail. "The buffalo just goes wild if it does not get "khaini" on time. It gets a strong urge for "khaini" and if not provided immediately, it starts throwing tantrums to get magic powder. Munda, adding if left free, it wanders around four miles looking for it and return only after consuming some of it. The buffalo has become talk of the village Khivri Khijri in the district. "It was also taken aback in the beginning because I could not understand sudden change in its behaviour. It used to go wild. Then talked to its past master who told me the buffalo is a "khaini" addict, Munda said. Interestingly, the "connoisseur" refuses to accept raw tobacco. It wants the "khaini" to be properly rubbed and duly patted with lime. If somebody rubs tobacco in front of the buffalo, it cannot resist the temptation and follow the human addict till it gets quota. The khaini-addict buffalo has certainly given some heady fodder for thought to its master. Buffalo refused to be milked without BBC? BBC is an acronym for ***Buddhi Bardhak Choorn, also known as "Khaini".***

A Child laughs so much that he starts crying; he laughs so deeply that the laughter becomes tears, tears come out of him. Laughter should be deep and total.

2. 'Cow' resolution leaves Punjab House staff in a fix

After the Punjab Assembly made an obituary reference to cows, allegedly slaughtered a bone crushing factory at Joga village in Mansa district, the Vidhan Sabha staff is in quandary over whom to send the formal condolence message. As per normal practice, condolence resolutions adopted in the Assembly are normally sent to the next of kin of all those are paid tributes during the obituary references at the opening of each Assembly session. Chief Minister Prakash Singh Badal later also declared that a memorial would be set up for the slaughtered cows. The project is likely to cost around ₹2 crore.

3. Seating problems

The Fifth SAARC Conference of speakers and Parliamentarians in New Delhi posed a tricky problem for Lok Sabha Speaker Meira Kumar. Faced with an embarrassing number of empty seats in Central Hall, she could have opted for an adjournment for lack of quorum had it been an ordinary session of Parliament. However, this being the inaugural ceremony of the SAARC event, she obviously did not have that option. She had to look for some other quick-fix solution, so the staff of the Lok Sabha was promptly parked among the audience to save the day for their boss.

4. 11.11.11 good day for divorce too

Mumbai: As droves of couples queued up at the marriage registrar's office to read their sacred vows, barely a kilometer away in Bandra, the family court too was abuzz with activity. The court received 32 applications on 11.11.11 from warring couples seeking, among other things, divorce, maintenance or

---

A day without laughter is a day wasted – *Charlie Chaplin.*
Laughter is one of the greatest helps to digestion – *Hufeland.*

---

protection from domestic violence. Even lawyers were taken by the special 'lucky' day. With the rush to file litigation reaching a high, a few advocates vetoed their clients' wishes for divorce. "This was such a happy day with many couples getting married, babies being delivered. We refused to file applications on November 11. We asked our clients why they wanted to break their marriage while the world was celebrating." said advocate Sadhana Jayakar-Lalwani.

5. My 'Boss is worst' a common feeling: Survey

Mumbai : Employees across the globe, including India, feel that, bosses are ineffective and lack empathy, or even the leadership skills, an international survey says. " About 68% want to change their job only because of their manager's attitude, 34% don't consider their manager to be effective at his or her job and only 40% reported that their boss never damages their self-esteem," says talent management firm DDI's report.

6. Marriages without sex now an epidemic says High Court

Pressure of urban living conditions taking its toll on couples'

A Marriage without sex can be reduced into an "insipid" relation. The Delhi High Court noted this as it expressed concern about the increase in number of divorces filed by urban couples claiming "sexual incompatibility and absence of sexual satisfaction". Justice Kailash Gambhir said lack of sex among married couples is becoming an "undeniable epidemic" due to the pressure of urban living conditions on couples. The decree was granted in favour of the man, who alleged that his wife did not maintain normal sexual relationship with him. "In the span of one year and two months of the married life, the couple had sex only about 10 to 15 times, Also, denial by the woman for sexual relationship on the very first night of the marriage is a grave act of cruelty as healthy sexual relationship is one of the basic ingredients of a happy marriage." contended the husband. He claimed his wife refused to participate in various traditional ceremonies. Earlier, the trial court had accepted his contentions and passed a divorce decree, but the woman moved the High Court challenging this order.

Finding substantial reasons to uphold this verdict, Justice Gambhir cited several judicial pronouncements on the issue and said it was a settled proposition that sex is the foundation of marriage, and that willful denial of sexual intercourse without reasonable cause would amount to cruelty.

"There has to be a healthy sexual relationship between a normal couple, but what is normal cannot be put down in black and white. Although it is difficult to exactly lay down as to how many times any healthy couple should have sexual intercourse in a particular period of time, as it is not a mechanical but a mutual act, however, there cannot be any two ways about the fact that marriage without sex will be an insipid relation," said Justice Gambhir.

The court said the frequency of sex cannot be the only parameter to assess the success or failure of a marriage, but it is unequivocal that "marriage without sex will be anathema".

Quoting a Bible verse, Justice Gambhir said: "That the twain shall become one flesh, so that they are no more twain but one is the real purpose of marriage and sexual intercourse is a means, and an integral one of achieving this oneness in marriage."

A good laugh is a sunshine in a house – *William Makepeace.*
Laughter is a good exercise.

---

7. 90% of Indians are fools: Justice Katju

Press Council of India chairman, Justice (retd) Markandey Katju said that a majority of Indians vote on caste or communal lines. "Ninety per cent of people in India are fools. Their minds are full of superstitions, communalism and casteism. They elected Phoolan Devi to Parliament since she belonged to a backward caste."

8. Former Judge gets 3-year jail term for taking bribe 26 years ago

New Delhi: A former Judge was sentenced to three years in Jail for taking ₹2,000 as bribe 26 years ago. With the court saying that a judge's ethical firmness is the need of the hour for society as people's confidence in Judiciary is getting shattered by the day.

Former judge Gulab Tulsiyani, 74, was handed down the jail term by Special CBI Judge V K Maheshwari who held him guilty of demanding and accepting illegal gratification for disposal of a factory challan case in 1986 during his tenure as a metropolitan magistrate at a Patiala House court here.

9. Hillary's gift full of mistakes

Kolkata: Even Rabindranath Tagore, who did not stick to conventional spellings, would perhaps not have permitted the bloomers that appeared on the mat that US secretary of state Hillary Clinton presented West Bengal chief minister Mamata Banerjee. Officials at the American Center did not respond to queries about the origin of the gift. The mat had Tagore's face at the centre. On the edges, words from one of his well-known songs - Aguner Poroshmoni Choaow Praney (Hold the magic stone of fire to the heart) – were inscribed. The word 'poroshmoni' was wrongly spelt.

While the next line should have been E. Jibon Punyo Koro (Grace this life), in place of the word 'punyo' it was written 'rinyo'. To make things worse, as common a word as 'jibon' was also incorrectly spelt. 'Extreme care and caution should have been exercised in such instances, said Sahitya Academi president and noted poet Sunil Gangopadhyay. This came on the eve of Tagore's birth anniversary, something patronized by Banerjee, who is greatly devoted to the poet.

10. Kid Killed kid just for a mango in Siwan

Siwan: Picking up a mango from a village orchard led to the gruesome muder of the five-year-old child, Sahil, in Siwan. 'The alleged murderer was not only a minor from the same village but also a distant relation of the victim as well'. And the reason: He wanted to eliminate Sahil just to teach him a lesson for pocketing some else's fruit.

11. Mota Mall & Chhota Maal

Minister advises officers to be moderate in corruption.

UP's PWD minister Shivpal Singh Yadav, CM Akhilesh Yadav 's uncle, recently advised officers in Etah to practice moderation in corruption.

The minister told the assembled officers that if they worked hard to give benefits like potable water to the people, they would be quite justified in stealing "a little bit" but should not fall prey to the temptation of becoming "dacoits" and indulging in "big loots." It is not known whether the PWD minister is familiar with the works of Aristotle. But the mantriji's view on

---

A laugh, to be joyous, must flow from a joyous heart, for without kindness there can be no true joy** – Carlyle.* ***Don't make me laugh.

---

corruption in moderation would seem to chime with the Greek philosopher's advocacy of the Golden Mean, which implies that a little bit of almost everything you might fancy is good for you, but an excess of anything is bad. In other words, while 'mota maal' – to use a term much in use in current political discourse – is unacceptable, what might be called 'chhota maal' may judiciously be winked at as an excusable indulgence.

Going by what deserves to be called the Yadav principle of moderation, the problem is not so much corruption as conspicuous corruption. In other words, a little chai-paani' is fine. But don't turn 'chai-paani' into the equivalent of the Queen's tea party in Buckingham palace, as 'Moderation' Clive might have said.

12. School to produce political leaders coming up

Thiruvananthapuram: India's First school for producing political leaders of tomorrow is taking shape in Kerala, opening up a career option for which education has never been mandatory. The Indian Institute of Political Management, coming up Thiruvananthapuram is planning to offer four masters degree programmes - political management, legislative affairs, strategic public relations and coalition management.

A brainchild of Kerala born IT entrepreneur Vinson Palathingal who is based in the United States, the institute will be an autonomous body under the state higher education department.

What's more, senior politicians and retired bureaucrats are on board to impart some lessons.

13. Hinglish has 'principles' in shock and awe

Ara: When Sheo Shankar Singh, Principal of Maharaja College, Ara, asked a student to write an application in English, What he got, actually knocked him out – flat.

The punch was too much. Boy scribbled: "Respected father, pranam your feet. I am well and you also well." Frustrated, he virtually shoved him out of his room. Singh is not alone. Other principals have confessed to being equally frustrated with the inability of today's students to write basic, error free English.

While Singh is now busy organizing 'Mind your language' counseling session for his students, others are having problems with students who cannot even read English.

Janeshwar Singh, Principal of HD Jain College, said, "Only 10% of all application received are grammatically correct and most so, when they are written by someone else. Otherwise, it plain disaster." He recalls, how a student explained his late coming saying, "Sir. My scooter understanding tree. No breeze, front wheel"!

Lalit Sagar, Principal of Jagjiwan College, laughed when he recalled, how a student of political science came to ask him, when the practical for the subject would be held!

Meera Srivastava, Principal of DAV school, admitted that 'several students write incorrect spelling in the applications. Some write 'principle' for 'principal', she said.

Most like Madhu Sinha, believe that lack of reading, fall in standards of teachers at early stages and lack of guardianship were some aspects, which had led to this sorry state.

A maid that laughs is half taken – *English proverb.*
Laughter may boost the immune system.

---

14. Little boy upstages Pope

Pope Francis was delivering a homily but a little boy stole the show. He was speaking in St. Peter's Square about the role grandparents play when a little boy walked up behind him and confidently sat down on the pontif's chair. Acting like an indulgent grandpa, Francis let the boy explore the area undisturbed before thousands. The Pope smiled while reading his speech as the boy sat in the chair, gazed up at him and at one point clung to the pontiff's legs.

15. Jairam says toilets more important in India than temples

Toilets are more important in India than temples, Union Minister for Rural development Jairam Ramesh said, as he inaugurated a yatra that will travel through states raising awareness about sanitation.

"Sixty-four per cent of Indians defecate in open spaces, which are a global record. It is now reckoned as the main cause of India's malnutrition problem. In the past five years, we have spent more than ₹45,000 crore on rural sanitation and will spend ₹1.08 lakh crore in the next five years to make India open-defecation-free country," Ramesh told a gathering of panchayat-level workers, children and officials.

16. Dead man 'helped' to marry live in partner

Rosya (Banka): Formalizing a live-in relationship by marriage after the death of one partner is an unheard of thing. But a small community of Santhals of Jaipur on Jamui's borders with Jharkhand, did just that. In doing so, they actually arranged century's old norm Ghotul, practiced in tribal regions, where

A real laugh is just like a small child laughs. Watch his belly shaking, his whole body throbbing with it – he wants to roll on the floor. It is a question of totality.

young adults live and cohabit, till they are sure, that the partners they may have chosen, are indeed good enough for marriage.

Chudki Hembrom and Mahalal Marandi, a daily wage earner, started living together ten years ago at an early age, as per the Ghotul norms and with the sanction of the community. However, they could not decide on marriage, due to poverty, which did not allow for the cost of the feast they would have to arrange for the whole community. During the period that they stayed together Chudki gave birth to two sons and two daughters. But even as they were finalising wedding rituals, Mahalal died, placing Chudki in the unenviable position of a pariah.

That is when the community stepped in. With the blessings of the community elders and the Shaman, it was decided, that before cremating Mahalal, the two should marry first! The community arranged for the rituals and the feast. A dead Mahalal's finger was used to put vermillion in Chudki's partings followed by the feast and later, the erasing of the mark of marriage and declaration of her widowhood. In doing so, the santhals upturned a long tradition, altering law, which would not have been practical in the present circumstance and thereby, set a precedent to help a young unwed woman with children.

Chudki told HT, the live in relationship was formalized at the advice of senior members of the village to ensure that her children have legitimate status. She said she willingly agreed for application of vermilion by her partner after his death as she was also keen, that none should refer to her children as illegitimate.

Chhabu Hembrom, father of Chudki, is happy that the elder of the community changed the tradition to help his daughter. He

---

After sadness is released, you will see laughter is arising. And after laughter has gone, you will feel light, weightless, flying.

---

said, "Had they not helped, it would have deprived Chudki from staking claim to the small piece of land that Mahalal left behind and she would have been outcast."

Shyamlal Tudu, Pradhan (headman) of the village, said: "This is the first live in relationship to be formalized after the death of one partner. We are proud of our traditions. However, in this case, the decision was driven by humanitarian considerations to which, the entire village agreed. We are also proud of this".

17. How to get a holiday

Lawyers in the Ghaziabad court found a unique method to get an extended weekend. Valmiki Jayanti (October 29) was a holiday at most government offices in the state, but not for courts. The lawyers of the Bar association called a strike on the day and forced the few courts that were in session despite the call to stop proceeding. The reason. "We are striking because we do not have holiday on Valmiki Jayanti," a lawyer said. As many as 20 lawyers raised slogans for half an hour, went to courtrooms and left the premises after ensuring that no one was working. Mission accomplished.

18. All sub-judges in Punjab, Haryana flunk exam for superior judiciary

As indictments of the lower judiciary go, this one is pretty damning. Each and every sub-judge from Punjab and Haryana who sat for the qualifying exam for superior judicial service two months ago has flunked. Only two - one each from the general category and OBC - of 148 lawyers who appeared for the exam passed. All candidates-lawyers and sub-judges-were cleared in a preliminary test of objective-type questions to appear for the main written exam for appointment as additional district and sessions judges (ADJ). The exams were held in Haryana on October 2, 2012 and in Punjab on November 4, 2012. Results were declared on 8.12.2012. For the first time, Punjab and Haryana High Court had set the main paper entirely on questions of law requiring only long-form, analytical answers. 38 sub-judges from Haryana and 26 from Punjab appeared – and failed. The Haryana topper among sub-judges scored 269 out of 600 marks, or 45%. The next highest scores were 180 (30%) and 167 (28%). The sub-judge who topped in Punjab scored 282 (47%), and was followed by candidates who scored 281 and 266 out of 600. Among the lawyers-who wrote a slightly different, 750-mark test – 146 failed? There were 20 law officers among them, including additional district attorneys and district attorneys, officers who appear for the state in lower courts.

Several judges blamed their "busy schedules" that had apparently kept them from preparing; others complained that the marking was "too strict". One candidate conceded, "The questions were not difficult or out of syllabus. They were based on latest laws." No candidate was willing to come on record.

Over two dozen posts of ADJs are vacant in Punjab and Haryana. "A fresh examination will have to be conducted. It was not expected that nobody will be able to clear the examination." Said a senior official of the high court."

19. 'Dented, Painted' Holy Cows

RSS chief says rearing gau mata will prevent attacks on women.

Speaking at a function organized to lay the foundation stone of what is billed as the country's first cow sanctuary, situated in

Madhya Pradesh, the RSS leader attributed attacks on women to a "lack of values", which could best be corrected if everyone were to rear cows, "Cow is our mother. Service to cow is service to mankind, which in turn helps to build morals." Pronounced Bhagwat.

Addressing the gathering on the same occasion, chief minister Shivraj Singh Chouhan rued the fact that till now India has only had wildlife sanctuaries, but none for cows. "We decided to make a cow sanctuary because cow is the base of our culture," the CM added. Has India's holy cow become an endangered species, like the Indian tiger, and is it in need of special protection? A quick reconnaissance of any street in any Indian town or city will reveal that far from being in danger of imminent extinction cows, holy or otherwise, are all too evident everywhere you look. The moo the merrier seems to be the disorder of the day. Stray cows act as mobile traffic islands around which cars, buses and two-wheelers swerve, horns blaring. Urban cattle act as living garbage disposal units, eating plastic bags for want of other nourishment. The moral of the story is that the cow is both India's most loved animal, and the animal that India most loves to exploit.

20. (12.12.12) - Big plans for 'special date'

New Delhi/Mumbai: Expectant Parents are trying to grab the last opportunity of the century to have a baby on 12.12.12, with gynaecologists being inundated with requests that the child be delivered on this special day.

"Would-be parents are even ready to advance or postpone the delivery date in order to make their child's birth special," said Dr Archana Dhawan Bajaj, Consultant gynaecologist at The Nurture Clinic at Naraina in west Delhi.

Babies have ability to laugh before they ever speak.
Laughter reduces your pain.

In Mumbai, businessman Navnit Chudasama, who is launching a construction company, is set to open the bank account for his new business on Wednesday (12.12.12). "It's a lucky day and I will try to arrange it at 12:12 pm to make it special," he said. Rohan Sharma (name changed on request), 15, will undergo a bariatric surgery to shed about 60 kg from his 126 kg frame.

21. Award for Bihar's Growth model

Deputy Chief Minister Sushil Kumar Modi would receive an award from President, Pranab Mukherjee at a national industrial and commercial convention to be held in New Delhi. The award is being given by Punjab and Haryana Chamber of Commerce and industry on selection of Bihar as 'the state with highest industrial growth.

22. Thirty (30%) of the accused in rape cases were neighbours of victims: Study

New Delhi: Over 30 per cent of the accused in rape cases are neighbours of the victims, a study conducted by police after the gang rape of a 23-year-old woman has revealed. The police study, which showed that 25 per cent of the accused were friends of the victims, also found that almost 90 per cent of the cases took place in homes, which the force cannot prevent. The study comes in a year the number of rapes in the capital has reached a record high (661 till December 15, 2012).

23. Train versus tortoise, is it?

New Delhi: If a Chinese train covering roughly 2300 km. in about 10 hours in one of the severest of cold conditions, makes headlines, the Indian Railways may well be in contention for the dubious distinction of running the slowest trains. Slumberous

Bangalore has the highest number of laughter clubs. Laughter reduces your weight.

speed: A train has been running at a slumberous speed of about 10 km. per hour in this age of bullet trains. It has been delayed by as many as 116 hours and 27 minutes. The 12488 Delhi-Jogbani Express is on the tracks for five days now having started its crawl on December 23, 2012. As per the projection it is likely to take about 139 hours and 43 minutes to cover the journey of 1383 km. running at the rate of 10 km. per hour. The tortoise, according to information posted on the internet, covers about 0.21 km. to 0.48 km. per hour.

Five times late: Normally the Delhi-Jogbani express is supposed to take about 23 hours and 16 minutes to reach its destination, almost less than a day. Now it is running almost five times behind its scheduled time.

24. She swallowed coin as child, retrieved it 24 yrs later

Mumbai: Twenty-four years ago, as a child, Ratna Ahire had swallowed a 10 paisa coin. She got rid of it just the other day. The doctors at Parel's KEM Hospital were stumped when Ahire, 29, turned up two months ago. There wasn't much that seemed wrong with her, yet she complained of being unable to eat. An X-ray found nothing. Then Ahire remembered the coin-swallowing episode. "in a bid to hide the 10 paisa from my siblings, I had kept the coin in my mouth and accidentally swallowed it. When I told my mother, she fed me bananas, assuming it would come out with the stools," said Ahire. There was no further complaint and Ahire forgot about the incident. "Nine years ago, after my wedding, I experienced some difficulty in swallowing food, but I ignored it. But the problem suddenly became acute two months ago. I could not eat anything and my husband insisted that I go to a hospital," said Ahire. "Usually we have children coming in with coins stuck in food pipes.

Beasts can weep when they suffer, but they cannot laugh – *Dryden.*
Laughter strengthens the body's ability to fight disease.

But such a case, where it has been stuck for so many years, is a first, "said Dr Aparna Deshpande, Professor of surgery, KEM Hospital. It took a multi-disciplinary approach and a team of 20 doctors from surgery, Gastroenterology, ENT and anesthesia to unstuck Ahire. The coin had corroded badly and tissue had grown around it, which had led to the difficulty in swallowing. Two endoscopic procedures had to be performed-one of them extremely tricky. Doctors said Ahire had been extremely lucky to have escaped a rupture in her food pipe. She had been lucky too, that it was a government hospital. Else, that 10 paisa would have burned a mega-hole in her pocket, instead of the meager ₹2,500 she spent on a CT scan.

25. Touching a chord

Musical Tribute: An ensemble of 600 guitarists plays John Lennon's Imagine, in memory of the 23-year-old Delhi gang rape victim, in Darjeeling.

26. 'Can't escape death and IT'

Actor Amitabh Bachchan, who has been issued a notice by the Supreme Court over tax dues, has reacted by saying, "Both death and Income Tax Department are inevitable in life." The apex court issued the notice on a petition filed by the Income Tax department, which claimed that the megastar owes to it ₹1.66 crore as taxes on income he earned through quiz show Kaun Banega Crorepati during 2001-02. "There are two things in life that one will have to face – death and I-T Department. Both are inevitable. In any case I will follow the Court's order," Bachchan said at the promo launch of the upcoming film Jolly LLB, a satire on Indian Judiciary. Asked if he ever had a bitter experience with the judiciary, he said, "No, not really. When my name cropped up during Bofors case in London, the only weapon I had was speaking the truth."

27. When Justice fled justice

Jabalpur: A sacked judge escaped from the district and sessions court here when he was about to be sentenced to a jail term in connection with the suicide case of his peon. Judge Nitish Kumare had been sacked from service after his peon committed suicide on February 27, 2010. At that time, Mr. Kumare was posted as Jabalpur judicial magistrate and had suspected that his peon Mohammad Niyaz had stolen ₹50,000 from him. Mr. Kumare beat Niyaz and also tortured him mentally, after which Niyaz committed suicide. On the basis of a suicide note, police registered a case against Mr. Kumare in Hanumantal police station.

28. Over 60 Harvard Students suspended for mass cheating

Boston: More than 60 students of Harvard University have been suspended and several others disciplined after being implicated in one of the largest cheating scandals that shook the Ivy League institution last year. The school implicated as many as 125 students when officials first addressed the issue last year. Half of the 279 students enrolled in an 'Introduction to congress' course were suspected of "academic dishonesty" ranging from "inappropriate collaboration to outright plagiarism" on a take-home exam. The class was widely seen on campus as an easy way to get a good grade.

Laughter tends to occur in short bursts vowel-like sounds such as "ha-ha, ho-ho or he-he", which are repeated every fifth of a second.

---

29. A priest, who drives an Audi, pays ₹10 lakh for fancy number

Chandigarh: He may preach renunciation to the world, but for Mahant Chotu Nath of Baba Gorakhanath dera in Chandigarh, ₹10.05 lakh is well spent on a fancy number for his luxury car of ₹55 Lakh Audi Q 7 SUV. He said, "My followers want me to travel only by car". The number – CH-01-AR-0001- he said was lucky for him. While the 23-year-old Mahant travels in style, he also uses an iPhone and has a 42-inch LED TV. Close Circuit TVs are installed in the entire dera- the control room being in his room that is plush with fancy couches. But when asked about his lavish lifestyle, he said, "I am a very simple person".

30. Sound Check

President Pranab Mukherjee, Prime Minister Manmohan Singh and Congress President Sonia Gandhi addressed an August crowd at Rashtrapati Bhawan but much of their speech went unheard, thanks to an extremely poor audio system installed in the Durbar Hall where the function was held. The event was organized to present the Indira Gandhi award for Peace, Disarmament and Development to Ela Bhatt of Ahmedabad-based NGO SEWA. Bhatt too could not be heard when she gave her acceptance speech. In fact, the noise of four pigeons that had entered the Durbar Hall was more prominent, compelling the President himself to look upwards to try and identify the culprit. Senior Rashtrapati Bhawan officials sheepishly acknowledged that the acoustics of the Durbar Hall had let them down and that they would immediately try and replace the sound system at the earliest.

Beware of too much laughter, for it deadens the mind and produces oblivion – *The Talmud.*

31. China executives forced to run half-naked for failing to meet targets

Beijing: Chinese firm made its employees, including women, to run half-naked in biting cold for failing to meet their targets, evoking criticism over the harsh rules of Chinese companies and the lengths they go in punishing their executives. State-run global times and several other dailies carried pictures of more than 10 men wearing shorts running in cold weather on a highway in Chengdu, the capital city of China's south-western province, Accompanying them were several women colleagues who wore thin clothes, Chengdu Business Daily reported. Chen, an office administrator at a food company, said the employees were being punished for falling short on their performance objectives. They all worked in the marketing department, she said. "We formed an agreement (with the employees) in the beginning of 2012. It stated that whoever fails to reach the goal must 'streak' on 3rd Ring Road. According to the agreement, women would run 5 km. wearing only shorts", Cheng said.

More than 20 employees went out into cold when temperatures were as low as 11°C.

32. Post retirement, Hillary to charge $200,000 per speech

Hillary Clinton has signed up for speaking circuit and will charge a whopping $200,000 per appearance, an amount more than her annual salary as the US Secretary of State. The $200,000 per speech fee will be a sizeable increase for 65-year old Clinton, who made $186,000 annually as secretary of state before stepping down.

Boy I am glad there is laughter after sad.
Laughter is the tonic, the relief, the surcease for pain – *Charlie Chaplin.*

33. UK to foreign Doctors: Speak Good English

London: From April, 2013 foreign doctors wanting to treat patients in UK hospitals run by the National Health Service (NHS) will have to prove they have the "necessary level" of English language skills, the government said.

34. Urdu paper shocker: 'Write a letter to brother informing about father death'

Pune: ***Aaapke waalid ke achanak inteqaal hone par apne chhote bhai ko taajiti khat likhiye...*** (write a brief letter to your younger brother informing him about your father's death.) (04 marks).

Shockingly, this was a question set for the Urdu language students of Class XII. The higher Secondary Certificate (HSC) examination in the state started from February 21, 2013. When these students appeared for their first paper, Urdu (Index No. 05), and attempted question No. 9 (B), some were visibly shaken while others were enraged.

Syed Saba, an Urdu teacher with Abeda Inamdar Junior College for Girls, Pune, said the question left many of her students " confused and nervous". Mushtaque Ahmed, a Class XII student, said, "The question left most of us amazed and confused. How can the board expect us to answer such a question? How can they ask us to imagine the death of our own father? I and all my friends attempted the optional question on writing to uncle about your plans for summer vacation."

35. Oldest marathon runner retires at 101

Hong Kong: 101 year old Fauja Singh, the world's oldest marathon runner of Indian-origin, retired from competitive

Children laugh about 400 times a day. Adults laugh an average of 15 times a day.

events as a "very happy" man as he finished his last race here. Singh, nicknamed the "Turbaned Tornado," finished the Hong Kong marathon's 10-kilometree race in 1 hour, 32 minutes and 28 seconds, but he could not meet his goal of beating his personal record of 5.40. "I'm very happy. When I was running I felt very good, but now that I've stopped, I'm tired," said the India-born British national, who only speaks Punjabi.

Singh, who turns 102 on April 1, 2013 became the oldest man to run a full marathon at Toronto in 2011. But his record was not recognized by Guinness World Records because he doesn't have a birth certificate to prove his age, only a passport. HUMBLE START: Singh, who was a farmer in Punjab before settling in England, has competed in nine 26-mile marathons in London, Toronto and New York. His best time was in Toronto, where he clocked five hours, 40 minutes and four seconds. Singh says he does not suffer from any physical ailments. A torchbearer for the London 2012 Olympics, his one regret is not being able to speak and read English.

36. Innocents abroad

New Delhi: There were some embarrassing moments during the goodwill visit to Australia in February, 2013 by a parliamentary delegation led by Minister of State for Parliamentary Affairs Rajiv Shukla. For instance, a woman MP from the DMK was asked to give the vote of thanks at one of the dinners. The MP was effusive in praising Lok Sabha Speaker Meira Kumar, the parliamentrary Affairs Ministry and the minister for having selected her for the trip. But she completely

***Children who are born blind and deaf retain the ability to laugh. Beware of him who hates the laugh of a child** – Lavater.*

forgot to thank the host country and her parliamentary counterparts from the other side for the dinner. A JD (U) MP got into a heated argument with the hotel staff because they could not understand his request for a "balti (bucket)" and a "mugga (mug)" for his bath. The management was equally puzzled about his request for "nimbu (lemon)" with hot water and the riddle could not be resolved even after he kept describing it as a "sour fruit". Finally, a fellow Indian was summoned to translate his instructions to the hotel manager.

37. Manipur HSC students get 'answered' question papers

Students appearing for a class XII board exam in Manipur were given question papers having answers printed on the back side, after which the test was cancelled. Hundreds of students were provided the question papers and blank answer sheets during the 'Engineering Drawing' exam organized by the Council of Higher Secondary Education, Manipur (CHSEM). After some examinees pointed out the error, invigilators collected the question papers and the exam was cancelled. CHSEM controller Sagolsem Kiran said he was surprised that it did not look like a printing mistake. An inquiry into the incident has been ordered, he said, adding that re-examination of the subject would be conducted on March 25, 2012.

38. Man mortgages daughters

In Andhra, father pledged girls with lender for defaulting on ₹34,000 loan.

Hyderabad: An impoverished father in Karimnagar district of Andhra Pradesh was forced to pledge his two minor daughters with a money lender for defaulting on a loan of ₹34,000. The

Commit to laughter. If you decide that you're going to laugh more, make yourself laugh at least once every day.

girls, aged 16 and 5, had a harrowing time for over three months as the money lender made them toil in the fields during the "bondage" period. The police said the older child even complained of molestation attempts by the money lender. What makes the case more tragic is that the money lender Nara Jahangir is the paternal uncle of the girls. The police rescued the girls on Friday following a tip-off about the girls' plight by one of the villagers. The girls' father told a local news channel that they had borrowed ₹34,000 from Jahangir six months ago to meet some urgent family needs but could not pay in time. Jahangir was pressuring him to repay the loan and had even threatened him. To get Jahangir off his hack he agreed to leave the two girls as "security" with him. "We have arrested Jahangir, he was produced in a court today and sent to judicial remand," Karimnagar SP Viswanath Ravinder told HT. The children were handed over to the district child protection officer, the SP added. Jahangir, a blacksmith, has been booked for bonded labour, wrongful confinement and criminal force on women with intent to outrage their modesty, the SP said.

39. Girls should have right to last rites: Cariappa

Dharhara (Vaishali): Prema Cariappa, Chairperson of Central Social Welfare Board said "Girls must be allowed to perform the last rites of their parents."

She also advocated that a family culture must be promoted to allow married couples to work together for rapid house hold economic growth.

Advocating that women should stand up boldly for change, she said, that would ring in the most effective initiative to bridge the gender gap".

Don't carry a serious face everywhere, and suddenly you will find a deeper health arising in you – deeper sources of your health become available.

---

40. Justice for minors lost in translation

New Delhi: A 13-year-old domestic help beaten by her employees used sign language to communicate with the policemen and welfare workers recording her statement. The tribal girl from Jharkhand spoke neither Hindi nor English and was not provided with an interpreter.

In another instance, the court case of a 15-year-old West Bengal girl, rescued from the capital's notorious GB road red-light area, was delayed as her interpreter was rejected on grounds of being 'influenced' and a replacement had to be found.

Language barriers and lack of interpreters/translators are leading to such court cases –of children who end up victims of sexual or physical abuse after being trafficked from across the country – pilling up and going nowhere.

41. Gujarat IPS officer files dowry case against her Dy. Collector husband

Surat: A probationary IPS officer posted as assistant superintendent of police at Valsad has filed a complaint of dowry harassment against her husband who is deputy collector of Behror in Rajasthan. Police said Sarojini Kumari, a 2011 batch IPS officer, married Narsingh Hajarilal, a Rajasthan Administrative service officer, in June 2011. After she was posted in Gujarat a few months ago, her husband started demanding dowry and used abusive language to threaten her. He also wanted her to quit her job. "Ours was love marriage. Even before our marriage, we had fights. But since we were in love, I tried my best to forgive and forget his misbehaviour. After marriage, he continued misbehaving with me and my family. He also used to assault me and did not want me to serve in Gujarat.

Don't worry about the sound of your laugh. Everyone's laugh is unique. Laughter will sit on the men of wit.

---

42. Bulls hanged for damaging crops

Bhopal: A day after a bull gored a man to death in Ghaziabad, three farmers angry with two bulls for rampaging through their fields hung the animals to death from a tree in Shivpuri district of Madhya Pradesh. The incident occurred at Mayapur village-around 10 km. from the district headquarters. Tension soon gripped the area when villagers spotted the bulls hanging outside the government middle school. "The owner of the bulls, Ram Lal has lodged a complaint with us," K.P. Sharma, assistant sub-inspector of Mayapur police station told TOI sand added that this was the first such crime reported in the area. Sources say that the bulls had strayed into the field of farmer Darshan Singh, causing huge loss to his crops.

This reportedly infuriated Singh so much that he caught the bulls with the help of his relatives and beat them with iron rods. Later they dragged the animals to the school building and hanged them to death- as a 'punishment' for causing the damage, the police said.

43. Indians vote like cattle Says Katju

New Delhi: India is not a full-fledged democracy as 90% of its people vote like sheep and cattle, Press Council of India chairman Justice Markandey Katju said. Ex-SC judge said that he would not vote as India was being run by leaders elected on the basis of their caste, which is not the true form of democracy. "I won't vote because my vote is meaningless. votes are cast in the name of Jats, Muslims, Yadavs or Harijans, Democracy is not meant to be run like this, Why should I waste my time in joining the cattle queue?" he asked.

Drama is hard for me. Crying is much harder for me than laughter – *Emma stone.*

---

44. Locked and loaded: Malik gifts Shinde Vintage gun

New Delhi: Some might say it's a case of Pakistan pointing a gun at India while others see it as an instance of accidental fire. Believe it or not, Pakistan's interior minister Rehman Malik, who visited India in December, 2012, gifted a non-firing vintage gun to his counterpart Sushil Kumar Shinde – a curious gift especially since LeT chief Hafiz Saeed and terrorism were high on the bilateral agenda. "We informed the ministry of External affairs that the minister desires to deposit the gun in the government treasury", an officer in Shinde's office confirmed when asked about the gun, adding, ' Antiques are not evaluated." If Shinde wanted to keep the gun, he would have had to acquire a license under the Arms Act. Asked about the curious choice of a Pakistani home minister carting a weapon as a gift, especially when terrorism is top priority on the bilateral agenda, the officer in Shinde's office said, "We can't control their intentions. Let the matter rest with the fact that it was an antique piece and a non-firing weapon."

45. Cop banks on astrologer for cracking loot case!

Patna: One often gets to hear of people resorting to exorcism and occult practices to get rid of evil spirits. Many critically ill in rural areas are often reported to be falling in the trap of exorcists who claim to have cure for all ills for persons in grip of evil spirits. But strangely enough, now even the police seem to be falling for it in this era of modern policing and scientific investigation. In the biggest ever bank loot incident involving ₹25 crore, a policeman got so desperate after failing to achieve any major breakthrough that he decided to take help of an astrologer of Haridwar. However, the astrologer first wanted to see the documents related to the case. For that to happen, the junior officer needed his senior's permission to take the documents to Haridwar. Unmindful of the repercussions, the junior officer approached a senior officer in the police headquarters for permission. This was enough for the senior to fly into a rage. "What nonsense! You are a police officer and will remain only that." Shouted the senior officer. The junior officer got the message and dropped the idea of astro help instantly.

"The prime objective is to crack the case and recover the money. Perhaps, instead of following the planetary movements, numerology, palmistry, the answer should be sought through criminology," he added.

46. J&K Minister Slaps Official For Being Late

Jammu: State home minister Sajjad Kitchloo allegedly slapped a senior administrative official and let his aides beat him up for arriving a few minutes late for a meeting. "I was late by about three minutes," said Riyaz Ahmad Choudhary, Chief Executive Officer of Kishtwar Development Authority. "The minister was furious. He made derogatory personal remarks and then slapped me twice." Choudhary said when he resisted the third slap. Kitchloo ordered the police to arrest him. "His men started beating me up I thought I may not come out alive. Officials of my department finally rushed in and rescued me with the help of the police." Choudhary has filed a complaint with the local police. The meeting was meant to fine-tune the preparations for chief minister Omar Abdullah's visit to the city.

47. Delhi airport's top dog calls it a day

New Delhi: In a few days, the curtain will come down on an illustrious 10-year career. As officers gather to toast him the senior most member of a team entrusted with your safety at Indira Gandhi International Airport will walk away – with a wag of his tail.

It could all have panned out differently for Amar, a black Labrador. If he had joined the army, he might have won commendations from Generals. Or fate could have let him grow to portliness as a domestic pet. But he was destined to make history. He was just one year old in 2003 when he became the first dog in airport security in Delhi. Over the next decade he did his job well enough to inspire his employers, the Central Industrial Security Force (CISF), to expand the team to 15-all but one of them Labradors like himself.

Delhi airport's top dog calls it a day. "Amar loves chicken so we have decided we will bear the cost of his food as a post-retirement benefit," said CISF official. A send-off is planned, with senior officials in attendance. And then the dog with the expert sniff will walk off into the sunset, snout held high.

48. Thirty-eight (38%) Indian tourists pocket hotel items

New Delhi: A global survey by an online accommodation booking service has revealed that 35% of the global travelers have no qualms about taking home hotel amenities.

49. Jharkhand village that doesn't milk its cows

Saraikela : In 21st century India, there is a village in Jharkhand that does not milk its cows, Superstitious, people of Chaura village – a nondescript hamlet in Seraikela – Kharsawan district – have been buying milk from neighbouring villages despite each family having at least two cows.

"We have not milked our cows for at least 150 years," Says Kunaram Hansda, 70. "My father used to say a priest had warned the villagers not to milk the cows" he said, adding, "those who dare to defy the diktat suffer physically and mentally." Local lore has it that some ancestors had killed two black cats for sneaking up to their kitchens and emptying the milk pots. Days later, several villagers fell sick as 'the cats' sprits' lay a curse on the village. Thereafter, goes the story, anyone consuming the milk of their cows would fall ill.

Another villager Mukesh Hansda said, "When some villagers tried to milk their cows the milk turned red." But this is only the stuff of a legend for Mukesh has never seen it happen, as none among his generation, he claims, has tried to test the story on its merit. Till then the 150-odd families of Chaura keep the business going for milkmen in nearby villages.

50. Mothers name their newborns to remember China earthquake

Beijing: Mothers in quake-hit areas in southwest China named their newborns with characters such as "luck" and "quake" to mark their births after the devastating earthquake. Another baby girl born in that hospital was given the pet name "Lutian", or "open air". With the help of her families and medical staff, Lu was painstakingly moved to a lawn outside the building, where she gave birth to the girl about two hours later. "The last character of her given name would be 'ping' of the word 'pingan' (meaning safe or peace), as we wish her a

Everybody laughs the same in every language because laughter is a universal connection – *Yakov Smirnoff.*

peaceful life, and never again will she experience disasters like this," said the baby's grandmother. Zhang Jing, who delivered a girl on Monday morning named her baby "yuanyuan", meaning destiny or luck.

51. Meghalaya Varsity gives 434 Ph.D. degrees in one year, faces probe

A PRIVATE university in Meghalaya has created a record of sorts: it has awarded Ph.D. degrees to as many as 434 candidates in 2012-13 academic year, even as only 10 of its faculty members have doctorates. In fact, according to an advertisement put out by the CMJ University, Meghalaya's first private state university set up in 2009, one can even approach a dental clinic in Panchaula for applying for a Ph.D. degree from the varsity. Varsity gives 434 Ph.D. in one year, faces probe. While the university awarded 434 Ph.D. degrees during 2012-13, 490 more were enrolled for its Ph.D. programmes in the same period.

52. Rum run

The Indo-Tibetan Border Police, which guards India's borders with China, is cheering. The Home Ministry recently decided to sanction the same amount of rum to ITBP personnel as their counterparts in Army are entitled to. The ITBP personnel, who have to work in extreme weather conditions, had been making this demand for quite some time now.

53. Shocking bureaucratic bungling

The recent judgment of the Supreme Court which commuted the death sentence of the Assam murder convict Mahendra Nath Das to life term reveals starling facts. President A P J

***Face laughs the same in every language because laughter is a universal connection** – Yakov Smimoff.*

Abdul Kalam had recommended clemency for him in September 2005. No material was produced by the Union that it had asked President Kalam to review his decision. Thereafter, in 2010. The Home Ministry sent a recommendation to President Pratibha Patil to reject Das's mercy petition along with a note from the then home minister P Chidambaram. Curiously the ministry did not append President Kalam's views. This lacuna was held to be incurable by a bench of the Supreme Court headed by Justice G S Singhvi. The bench found it 'most intriguing' that the final recommendation sent to President Patil did not make any mention of Prsident Kalam's opinion and thus deprived there of an opportunity to objectively consider the entire matter. The court further observed that the government had also failed to explain the time lag of three years, between 2011, when then home minister LK Advani recommended rejection of the mercy petition, and 2004 when the file actually reached Rashtrapati Bhawan. There was also inordinate delay of five years after Kalam favoured clemency in 2005, with the file sent back to Rashtrapati Bhawan in 2010. In the result, the death sentence was commuted to imprisonment for life.

Bureaucratic bungling is not uncommon. But in a matter of life and death of a person, it is unpardonable. Convict Mahendra Nath Das has fortunately been spared the gallows. But that should not preclude a full judicial inquiry into these shocking lapses.

54. CBI

CBI has become a caged parrot, speaking in its masters' voice. it is a sordid saga that it is one parrot with many masters...

CBI should know how to stand up to all pulls and pressures. Yours was an act of indiscretion...

Face new chuckles. When you're alone at your house, or when you're driving to work, try laughing a few times as realistically as you can.

How can joint secretary go through the probe report? Outsiders, whose roles are under the scanner, are allowed access to the reports and CBI calls it mere interaction...

It was an absolute mistake you should now admit your fault instead of justifying it that you had reasons to accept these changes.

55. Spirited bride dumps drunk groom

Giridih: A 20-year-old bride from Giridih district of Jharkhand walked out of the wedding mandap in a huff halfway through the rituals once she discovered that the groom was drunk. That is not all. The bride's family and the rest of the villagers backed her decision and in the end, the groom and his family were practically chased out of the place. "We have never seen such a badly behaved groom. As soon as he entered the wedding venue, he started using abusive words. He also got into a scuffle with senior members of our family," said the bride's elder brother, Santosh Thakur. By the time the rituals started, the bride also noticed the strange behaviour and refused to proceed with the garland exchange ceremony. The Bagodar police station officer in-charge Satish Kumar confirmed the incident but added that no FIR was lodged by either of the parties in this connection.

56. Signing blindly

In the Collegium to select a new member of the National Human Rights commission, Arun Jaitley and Sushma Swaraj disagreed with the majority's choice of Justice Cyriac Joseph. The minutes of the meeting approving the appointment were first signed by Prime Minister Manmohan Singh, Lok Sabha Speaker Meira Kumar, Home Minister Sushil Kumar Shinde and

---

***For a laugh, for laugh. Frequent and loud laughter is the characteristic of folly and ill manners; it is the manner in which the mob express their silly joy at silly things** – Chesterfield.*

Deputy Chairperson of the Rajya Sabha P J Kurien. When it came to the turn of the Opposition leaders to affix their signatures and attach their dissenting note, they discovered to their amazement that the ruling party members had all signed the minutes without even realizing that the place where Joseph's name had to be filled in had been left blank. An embarrassed government hastily withdrew the minutes and made a fresh document.

57. Charity

A beggar woman was sitting on the roadside, holding a child and weeping. Passer-by. "What is the matter. Why are you crying?" Woman: the baby and I are both starving. We have not eaten for two days because I have no money. The man searched in his pockets and brought out a ₹500 note. "I only have this note. You take it and go buy milk for your child and food for yourself, sufficient for the next two days. Return me the change. I'll stay here and look after your child," said the passer-by. The woman did as instructed, and returned the man ₹280 change. Passer-by (to himself): Charity is truly a wonderful thing. The baby has got milk, the woman has got food and I have got rid of that fake ₹500 note. (Contributed by Rajeshwari Singh, New Delhi.)

58. Parting Gift

On his visit to Thailand, Prime Minister Manmohan Singh brought a sapling of the Bodhi Tree from Bodh Gaya for the ailing King of Thailand. He was to visit King Bhumibol Adulyadej at his hospital, to hand over the sapling from the tree under which Lord Buddha is believed to have attained enlightenment. However, the King's health did not show the improvement that

***Give a child love, laughter and peace** – Nelson Mandela.*
Life is not serious. Only graveyards are serious, death is serious.

would have allowed him to meet visitors. The courtesy call had to be cancelled. Thus, Singh ended up giving the sapling to Thailand PM Yingluck Shinawatra.

59. Bihar bridges language gap

Students to learn Hindi equivalents of dialect words.

Beginning mid-July, 2013 teachers across 42,701 government primary school in Bihar will teach class one students Hindi equivalents for words in Bajjika, Maithili, Bhojpuri, Angika and Magahi dialects. While the state government describes this as a ***language bridge*** course, some call it a move to cater to linguistic aspirations and others term it mere "tokenism".

Students will be taught that Bajjika words pahun, mehraru and sanghatiya mean guest or brother-in-law, wife and friend, respectively; katek and pai in Maithili mean how many and money, respectively; chuliha newar in Angika means 'an invitation to all family members'; and nimman in Bhojpuri means good.

Bihar government claims to be the first state to start a ***'bhasha setu'*** or language bridge course. While the HRD cites "purely academic reasons" to launch the course, the move is also the first step of the government to acknowledge major dialects. Though a language bridge course was discussed in the national curriculum framework in 2005, Bihar claims to be the first state to give it a concrete shape after adopting it in 2008. The state government, which is getting dictionaries printed for this purpose. "As government schools have mostly students from villages, it's important to provide them a comfort level. They hardly speak Hindi. Teachers, with the aid of the dictionary, will help children to pick up Hindi words. The dialect of Hindi dictionary will be primarily for teachers but can be referred

God made both tears and laughter, and both for kind purposes; for as laughter enables mirth and surprise to breathe freely, so tears enable sorrow to vent itself patiently. Tears hinder sorrow from becoming despair and madness – *Leigh Hunt.*

to students as well. The idea is to minimize number of out-of-school children." Asked if the course was being introduced with political intentions, the official said. "it is based on purely academic considerations."

60. Carrying pregnant wife, Kerala tribal man walks 40 km. to hospital

Carrying his ailing seven-month pregnant wife on his back, a nomadic tribal youth walked for almost an entire day before he finally got a vehicle to take her to hospital, in Pathanamthitta district of Kerala. While he managed to save his wife, the couple lost their child. Ayyappan and his wife, Sudha, reportedly left their home in Konni forest. When Sudha could not walk after some time, Ayyappan fashioned a sling from a piece of cloth and carried her on his back.

While Ayyappan is not sure of the total distance he covered, he is reported to have walked about 40 kilometers. His wife was first taken into Pathanamthitta district hospital, from where she was sent to Kottayam medical college hospital.

"The woman's life could be saved, but the baby could not be saved. We induced labour for delivery of the dead foetus," Dr Kunjamma Roy, head of the gynaecology department at Kottayam medical college, said. When the woman was brought the hospital, she had oedema, high blood pressure and convulsions, Dr Roy Said.

61. Bar Council wants a say in judges' appointment

Demanding participation in the appointments of judges to the Supreme Court and the High Courts, the Bar Council of India, the apex lawyers' body in the country, has adopted a resolution

Laughter usually doesn't interrupt a sentence structure of speech. We really only laugh during the pauses we make for coughing or breathing.

to approach the Centre and others with a request to accord them a role in the existing collegiums system.

62. Kolkata headmaster held for molesting kindergarten kids

A headmaster of a private school in Kolkata was arrested for allegedly molesting three children of classes Upper KG and II. Bijoy Shaw has been accused of molesting the children for quite some time.

63. 'Religious men' held with ₹1 crore in stolen money

Rescuers working to evacuate stranded pilgrims claim to have recovered over ₹1 crore over the past two days from the last few batches to be airlifted, money that had apparently been looted from this devastated town.

The stolen jewellery and money, some of it in muddied and wet bundles of cash, amounts to ₹1.25 crore and will be dispatched soon to the district magistrate by the NDRF and ITBP.

Officials said many of those trying to make away with the loot were religious men or "babas", and were only caught because of some alert troopers. Given the offerings made at temples in the holy town, cash to the tune of crores changes hands on a regular basis.

The single bank that serviced the town has been washed away, as is the case with the cash registers and strong boxes in most shops and establishments. While the presence of personnel at the main temple has kept it relatively safer, donation boxes and treasure chests at other temples have been forced open. "What got us suspicious was that some 'babas' lined up for evacuation had with them stacks of fresh, unused notes, A quick search revealed that the notes were all numbered and probably belonged to a bank," a rescue personnel said.

"One of the 'babas' had ₹62,000 in cash hidden in a ***dholak (drum)***. Another had a packet of prasad that revealed ₹10,000 in sequenced notes. One had sewn ₹1.2 lakh into his clothes," another rescuer said. People are let off if the money appears to be their own – being of different denominations, and appearing well used.

A veteran official almost broke down while talking about one religious man who had an unusually large number of rings and bagles on his hand. A search revealed more such ornaments on his person. "He confessed that he had robbed pilgrims, even cutting off the fingers of a few."

64. Groom thrashed, 2nd marriage plan foiled

Gaya: When his marriage was fixed with a girl of Sherghati in Gaya district, Bablu did not reveal that, he was already married. He had to pay a heavy price for keeping his first marriage a secret. Unaware that his estranged first wife had played a spoilsport by disclosing about their 14-year old marriage to the family members of his would-be second wife, Bablu, a resident of Aurangabad district and members of his wedding party reached the bride's house at Hamzapur in Amas police station area of Sherghati to tie the nuptial knot. 'Shocked over the disclosure that Bablu was already married and had a 13-year-old child, the family members of the bride mercilessly thrashed the groom and some ***baratis*** (members of the marriage party).

Man is distinguished from all other creatures by the faculty of laughter** - Joseph Addison. **You can turn painful situations around through laughter.

The groom and the baratis were let off only after they agreed to bear all the expenditure of the wedding arrangements that came to around ₹50,000.

65. Name game: 3,626 villages named after Ram, 3,309 after Krishna

The Indian Express went through the names of all 6,77,459, inhabited and uninhabited, villages in India, as listed in census 2011- data for which was released recently. Lord Ram ranks way up there, with 3,626 villages named after him, in almost all parts of the country except Kerala, while Lord Krishna is a close second at 3,309.

There are 92 villages in the country whose names start with Bengal/Bangal and all of them are located outside West Bengal, including. Maharashtra, Punjab and Andhra Pradesh. There are 33 villages named Kerala outside the state, mainly in the northern parts. There are 17 villages in the name of Prayag (the old name of Allahabad) and 41 named Kashi (the old name of Varanasi). There are 28 Agras outside Uttar Pradesh (West Bengal and Assam) while 189 village names start with Bihar, of which 171 are outside Bihar. There are 28 villages named Dhaka (the capital of Bangladesh) and 40 in the name of Nepal.

Besides, there are 47 villages whose names start with Badri and 75 which feature Kedar – invoking the religious sites which were among the worst hit in the Uttarakhand floods. Most of these villages are located in Uttar Pradesh, Uttarakhand, Madhya Pradesh and Bihar.

Other Ramayana Characters too figure among the names, although Bharat (187 villages) 3,626 villages named after Ram is marginally ahead of Lakshman (160). Hanuman has 367

He deserves Paradise who makes his companions laugh – *Koran.*
He could move a cloud when he laughed aloud.

---

villages in his name, while Sita has 75. While at least six villages in the country exist in the name of Ravana, and three in the name of his father Ahiravan (all in Bihar), no village is named after Ravana's brother Vibheeshana who crossed over Ram's side. Some Villages in Karnataka and Andhra Pradesh are named Ayodhya. When it comes to Mahabharata, Krishna remains the popular choice by far. While there is no Kurukshetra (except Haryana's original Kurukshetra) Village in the country, only two villages are named after Yudhisthira, the symbol of truth. There are 385 named after Bhim, and 259 in the name of the other popular Pandava brother, archer Arjun. Only one village bears the name of the patriarch Bhishma and that is in Orissa's Ganjam district.

Jawaharlal Nehru figures in 72 village names, and there are 117 in the name of Mahatma Gandhi, While there is no village in the name of former PM Lal Bahadur Shastri, 13 are in the name of B R Ambedkar, 36 are named after Indira Gandhi and 19 after Rajiv. Among the Mughal emperors, Akbar tops the list at 234 villages. His grandfather Babur has 62 villages in his name while father humayun has only 30. Interestingly while 51 villages are named after Shahjahan, only eight are in the name of Aurangzeb (all in Bijnor district of U.P.).

66. HC rejects plea to cut court holidays: Overworked, why deny us vacation

A PIL seeking reduction in the duration of court vacations and cancellation of the months long summer break in the Delhi High Court prompted the Acting Chief Justice to ask the petitioner why he was against holidays for judges. The petitioner said vacations should be curtailed so that a large number of pending cases could be dealt with.

Man is the only creature endowed with the power of laughter; is he not also the only one that deservcs to be laughed at ? Greville.

"We will examine the issue but why are you against our holidays?' Acting Chief justice Badar Durrez Ahmed asked petitioner S P Manchanda, Presient of NGO Prakash India, who had appeared in person to argue the case.

The petitioner said long summer vacations "infringed on the fundamental right of the people to get speedy justice and was violative of Articles 14 and 21 of the Constitution".

The PIL sought orders to "discontinue the summer vacations of the High Court of Delhi" and to "curtail vacations of the Delhi High Court by 10 to 15 days as recommended by the Law Commission of India."

The petitioner argued that courts had huge arrears of cases, and several thousand cases were pending before the Delhi High Court. The solution he said, was to increase working hours and reduce the vacation time of the courts. "En bloc summer vacations are a concept introduced by the British who found the Indian summer unbearable. Why should it continue now when we have ACs and other technology that makes working in the summer easy?" Manchanda argued.

The bench of Acting Chief Justice Ahmed and Justice Vibhu Bakhru, dismissed the plea. Judges and lawyers are already overworked and cannot be required to work anymore than they already are. "If the court is sitting in rotation, when will lawyers get a break?"

The petitioner was told that the Delhi High Court was "religiously" following Central government rules mandating 210 court sitting days, and that judges had to do a lot of work even when they were not sitting in the courtrooms.

He laughs best who laughs last – *English Proverb.*
Her laugh broke like a dish – *Cynthia Ozick.*

"Most judges do not spend their summer vacations vacationing but spend time in their office at home or in High Court writing judgments, "the bench said.

"Perhaps the petitioner does not know that even in summer vacation, the court is not closed for those who are in urgent need, vacation benches sit every Monday, Wednesday and Friday," the bench said.

67. Rich prefer spending on lifestyle than charity activities; Report

New Delhi: Charity donations have suffered as the super-rich prefer to maintain their opulent lifestyle over philanthropy in the gloomy economic environment, a report by rating agency Crisil said.

68. Higher education in Bihar disappointing, says Meira

Darbhanga: Stating that the condition of higher education in Bihar, Uttar Pradesh and some other states was 'disappointing'. Lok Sabha Speaker Meira Kumar stressed on establishing institutional machinery to ensure that it was relevant to changing times. Kumar lamented that the number of illiterates in India was maximum in the world. "there is a big gap between literate and the well-to-do in urban areas and illiterate and deprived sections in villages. Similarly, there has been a gap between male and female literacy rate and also between states".

69. School a hut; children eat at rail tracks in Patna

Some 70 students of Rajkiya Prathmik Vidyalaya in Raj Nagar, Patna eat sitting on the tracks about 20 feet from their

---

He who has laughter on his side has no need of proof *– Theodor Adorno.*
He who laughs last laughs longest. Man thinks. God laughs *– Jewish Proverb.*

---

school, a thatched hut, all year round except when it rains. It isn't much relief that trains run on the line just once in the morning and in the evening. The children said they eat at the tracks because there isn't enough space at the school. "It is easy even for cooks to serve food. There are flat wooden logs to sit and keep our plates," said Class V students, adding that their teachers are fine with the arrangement.

The teachers insisted that they have tried to keep the children away from the tracks, but have had little success. "They know the train timings. It does not come during their midday meal time. Even their parents' reprimand does not help," one of the teachers said. Several parents agreed that it was dangerous for their children to sit on the tracks and eat but maintained that not much can be done until the government provides the facilities. "The track is too close to the school and the children cannot avoid using it," said Ram Sharan of Ajanta Colony.

70. Error makes Sikhs most jobless in cities

New Delhi: A statistical flaw has earned the Sikh community the dubious distinction of being most unemployed religious group in Indian cities.

The latest National Sample Survey Office (NSSO) survey had said that unemployment had risen among Sikhs in urban areas between 2004-05 and 2009-10 even though it dropped for all other religious groups. Around 4.6% of Sikhs were unemployed in urban areas in 2004-05. The percentage increased to 6.1% in 2009-10. However, during the same period the unemployment rate for Hindus and Muslims fell by one percentage point. The maximum fall was witnessed for Christians, whose unemployment rate fell from 8.6% to 2.9% between 2004-05 and 2009-10.

***Men show their character in nothing more clearly than by what they think laughable** – Goethe.*

The NSSO admitted that there can be a flaw in the estimation as the sample size for unemployed persons among Sikh community was very low as compared to overall worker people ratios.

71. Rise of women's pill as condom use falls

New Delhi: Indian women may finally be getting a say in planning their families. Latest government data shows a steep fall in the use of condoms but an increased use of woman's contraceptives.

"To me it means that women are taking control over their lives and deciding when they want the next baby," said Shailaja Chandra, the former Chairperson of the National Population Stabilization Fund. The fund aims to bring down the fertility rate by making contraceptives popular. But there is a different take as well. "Women may be forced to use these contraceptives as men have reservations against wearing condoms," said a ministry official, adding the data indicated that the government's family-planning programme was working as fertility rate had fallen. Typically, fall in condom use should have led to rise in the population but it didn't, as women took charge. "Most women have realized that pills are a safer option than condoms," said Dr Suneeta Mittal, head of gynaecology department at Gurgaon's Fortis Memorial Research Institute.

72. SSP 'kills himself' for daughter's quota seat

Chandigarh: A serving district police chief in Punjab had himself declared 'killed in terrorist action' so that his daughter could avail of the quota set aside for martyrs' kin, when she applied for an MBBS programme. The officer in question, Rajjit Singh Hundal, is the Tarn Taran SSP. The certificate issued by the office of Hoshiarpur deputy commissioner Varun Roojam in

Misery plus laughter, and you will not look so miserable ! It is misery plus seriousness that makes you look so miserable.

June, 2013 reads thus; "Certified that Sh. Rajjit Singh son of Sh. Ajit Singh is father of Ms Sukhmani Hundal who was killed in terrorist action in Punjab during terrorist operation of security forces acting in aid or civil power."

Admission norms mentioned in the prospectus of the university stipulate that 2% seats will be reserved for the "wards of terrorism/riot affected persons."

When Sukhmani applied for the MBBS programme offered by the Baba Farid University of Health Sciences, Faridkot, she produced this certificate. According to BFUHS sources, the fraud came to light during the scrutiny of Sukhmani's documents, part of the routine admission procedure. When HT got in touch with Hundal, he blamed the university. He said he had never declared himself dead, only claimed that he was from a terrorist affected family as his mother and sister were killed by terrorists in 1991, but the university had misunderstood him.

73. Grand farewell for ₹25L buffalo

Chandigarh: A Haryana Village is all decked up to give a grand farewell to a buffalo, which was recently sold for ₹25 lakh to a farmer from Andhra Pradesh. Owner of the buffalo, Kapoor Singh is a farmer and he invited over 2000 guests from across the state to witness the function at Singhwa Khas village in Hisar district. Singh has also made arrangements to provide lunch for all the guests. The farewell party is expected to cost him around ₹2 lakh. Special silver ornaments worth ₹25,000 have also been bought to deck up Lakshmi, which was the show-stopper buffalo at the Murrah catwalk two years ago in Jind. Lakshmi, adjudged the best buffalo at **Muktsar cattle fair** earlier this year (2013), has till now bagged prizes worth ₹3 lakh in milk yield and other contests. Sarpanch spotted her

He, who laughs best today, will also laughs last – *Friedrich Nietzsche.*
He who laughs last is the slowest to think. He who laughs last laughs best.

at **Muktsar cattle fair** in Punjab. One of its male calves was also sold for ₹3 lakh.

74. One lakh apply for 'one-way ticket' to Mars never return

Washington: The Mars one project by NASA which aims to colonize Mars beginning in 2022 has reportedly revealed that more than one lakh people are eager to join the project in a bid to visit the red planet, but do not want to come back.

75. In Orissa, a former king now depends on villagers for meals

There are no rusting swords or throne in his house. No trophies on walls to serve as reminders of his hunting trips. No yellowing photographs of his younger, glory days. The palace where he lived with his wife and children till 1960 now houses a girls' high school. All that 92-year-old Brajraj kshatriya Birbar Chamupati Singh Mahapatra, erstwhile king of Tigiria in Cuttack district, has is a mud hut with some plastic chairs. The asbestos roof is leaking. So a torn tarpaulin sheet covers his wooden cot. There are a few books, a plastic saline bottle, a torch, some raw tomatoes and lots of cobwebs. Estranged from his family, the former king now leads an impoverished life. While cataract has taken a toll on both his eyes, he finds it increasingly difficult to hear too. In puruna Tigiria village where he has been living alone since 1987, few know that he is the only surviving royal member of the 26 erstwhile kings of the princely states of Orissa who signed the merger agreement with India on December 15, 1947. Tigiria was the smallest of the

Hearty laughter is a good way to jog internally without having to go outdoors *– Norman Cousins.*

26 princely states of Orissa, with an area of just 119 sq km. with his place sold to the government for ₹75,000 in 1960, the former king turned-recluse now survives on the charity of his former subjects. "The villagers give him his meals every day. It's a lonely life for him," says Lalit Krishna Das, a local advocate.

Dharanidhar Rana, a villager, says Mahapatra is frugal eater. "He just takes tea and a couple of biscuits for breakfast, some rice and dal for lunch and a roti at night. He eats chicken once in a while," says Rana's daughter Champei. Clad in a lungi and kurta, as he walks with the aid of a stick, it is difficult to picture the bearded Mahapatra as a former king.

76. For new IIT, IIM faculty, the question: what will our spouses do

When professor Ashish Nanda Robert Braucher Professor of Practice at Harvard Law School- agreed to take the top job at IIM – Ahmedabad recently, a critical factor that influenced his decision was the availability of a reasonably good job for his dentist wife in the city. Dr Shubha Nanda, a leading dentist at Brookline, Massachusetts, is learnt to have done the rounds of the city with Prof Nanda, till she found a suitable post in a Gandhinagar dental college.

77. Australian doctors bring woman back from the dead

Sydney: An Australian woman has lived to tell the tale after being brought back to life from being clinically dead for 42 minutes, doctors said.

Mother-of- two Vanessa, 41, was rushed to Monash Medical Centre in Melbourne last week after a major heart attack, with

---

Here is some techniques for artificial laughter! Get up from your bed and stretch out your limbs as you yawn. Make the "Aaaaaaaaahaaaa!" add giggles, increase the volume until they become a full laughter.

---

one of her main arteries fully blocked. She went into cardiac arrest and was declared clinically dead. Doctors refused to give up and used a compression device called a Lucas 2 to keep blood flowing to her brain while cardiologist Wally Ahmar opened an artery to unblock it. Once unblocked, Tanasio's heart was shocked back into a normal rhythm. "Indeed this is a miracle. I did not expect her to be so well". Tanaslo said she had no history of heart conditions and was grateful to be alive." Clinical death is a medical term when someone stops breathing and his/her blood stops circulating.

78. Dead cow sparks clash in Indore, curfew clamped

Indore: A day before the Raksha Bandhan festival, 25 people, including 20 policemen, were injured in a communal clash in Chandan Nagar area of Indore. Curfew was clamped and 325 people detained after the clash in which at least two vehicles were torched and others damaged.

Trouble started in the morning when a carcass of a cow was found by the side of a nullah in Ambar Nagar. As news spread, a large number of people gathered and demanded action against those responsible. They blocked traffic, but lifted it following police intervention. But as the crowd began to disperse, they were reportedly pelted with stones. When the police tried to enter the lanes, they too were attacked. Police used tear gas shells and then fired at the mob to control rioting, but when the situation did not improve, a curfew was clamped.

79. Royal wedding to bring Patiala closer to Shimla

Two royal families forming a marital alliance isn't unusual but what sets this one apart is that it also brings together two

---

High laugh, like a dove cry *- Eudora Welty.*
Meaningless laughter is a sign of ill-breeding *- Arab Proverb.*

---

prominent political dynasties. For Himachal's old Bushahr state, represented by CM Virbhadra Singh, it ensures strong ties with Punjab's powerful Patiala royalty – though it may not signify much in this age.

Virbhadra's youngest daughter Aprajita Singh, 26, Currently pursuing Textile Designing and Management at Manchester in UK – is set to marry Angad Singh, her schoolmate and grandson of former Punjab CM Captain Amarinder Singh, the erstwhile Maharaja of Patiala. Angad, who was a class senior to her at Lawrence School in Sanwar, is the son of Jai Inder Kaur, Amarinder's daughter. His grandmother is Union MoS (External Affairs) Preneet Kaur. The engagement ceremony was held in New Delhi. While Virbhadra was present, Amarinder gave it a miss.

80. Now, a fixed 'pay-n-pass' literacy exam

Katihar: It is called the 'great examination' **(mahapariksha)**. Sadly, what happened at examination centres in Katihar bore not even a passing resemblance to greatness. Reporters, who visited the centres where the examination was going on for awarding 'complete literate' certificates to neo-literates under the Centre and Sate's joint **'saksharta abhiyan'** (literacy mission), were in for a shock. Many examinees, a number of them married women, confessed they were given answer sheets in which the answers had already been written by somebody else! Other sources claimed the Katihar experience, by and large, held true for the way the literacy examination was conducted across Bihar. "When I reached my designated examination centre, I was advised to return to my household chores with the promise the course completion certificate would be delivered to me," said an examinee, Rinki Devi of Korha.

His laughter was so contagious that whosoever heard it would start laughing. No one is laughable who laughs at himself *– Lucius Annaeus Seneca.*

Another examinee at the Rampur centre in Korha said the certificate was up for purchase. "Two persons told me if I paid ₹500, I would get the certificate even without appearing at the examination," he claimed.

At five examination centres covered by scribes in Korha, many examinees were found absent and hired persons, mostly regular students of high schools and colleges, were writing the papers on their behalf. At one centre, a teacher showed several answer sheets written in the same handwriting. "Everything is fixed with a group of persons writing the papers for all the examinees in the district," he confessed. Bihar's director, jan shiksha (mass education), Jitendra Prasad said he was not aware of any literacy examination irregularities. "It is just a 'motivational' course of six months duration for which a certificate is provided.

81. Retd. Lt. Col. sent in 15-day judicial custody

Chennai killing: Confesses to shooting 13-year-old says police, rifle used in the crime recovered from river.

Chennai: Kandasamy Ramraj, a former assistant engineer in the Small Arms wing of the Electrical and Mechanical Department, has confessed to the crime, and the US-made rifle that was used for the murder was recovered from the bottom of Cooum river where it was dumped after the incident last Sunday (9th July, 2011). The 58-year-old from Madurai, who retired in April and was on extension. K. Dilshan, a 13-year old boy who resided at a slum abutting the Old Fort Glacis Officers' Enclave at Island Grounds area in the heart of Chennai, was shot when he and his friends trespassed into the Army compound to pluck fruits (almond) as is wont for the children in the neighbourhood. The bullet from the 30 calibre M1 Springfield rifle pierced the

Humour is by far the most significant activity of the human brain *- Edward Bono.*
The person who can bring the spirit of laughter into a room is indeed blessed
- Bennett Cerf.

child's head and came out through the other side, causing a fatal injury that led to his death. According to the police, Ramraj said in his confession that he was annoyed by the neighbours frequent straying into the defence compound despite repeated warning. On Sunday (9th July, 2011) afternoon, standing in his balcony, an irked Ramraj shot at the boy scaled the compound wall, and left the residential compound on a car soon after. He then dumped the rifle for which he had taken licence in 2004, while he was posted in Jabalpur, Madhya Pradesh. The Fast Track Court has sentenced him life imprisonment. Also 3-years imprisonment and a fine of ₹60,000. Both the punishment will run concurrently. Out of ₹60,000, a sum of ₹50,000 will be paid to the Dilshan's family.

82. Bihari among 5 held with 5.5 kg. gold in intestines

Varanasi: Five smugglers carrying gold inside their bodies were on Tuesday (27.8.2013) arrested at Lal Bahadur Shastri Airport hereby official of the Directorate of Revenue Intelligence (DRI), New Delhi.

The smugglers, who arrived from Sharjah by a Spiicejet flight, were carrying a total of 5.5 kg. gold in their intestines. The yellow metal, meticulously concealed in condoms before being placed inside the bodies, was retrieved by medical staff later.

Those arrested have been identified as Shambhu Yadav, 34, a resident of Bihar and Rohit, Harish Kumar Yashpal and Rajendra Singh, all residents of Amritsar.

According to reports, after DRI officials got information about the smuggling, a two member team arrived at the airport in morning. Around 7am, the flight arrived and the smugglers alighted. However, even after intensive checking of their luggage the officials could not find gold. This aroused the suspicion of the officials. They then subjected all the five to an intensive body scan at the airport. It was only then that they came to know about the gold inside their bodies. After the arrest, the smugglers were immediately taken to the Deen Dayal District. Hospital for a complete body scan. At the hospital, doctors successfully retrieved the gold from their rectum. A senior doctor said the smugglers had hidden the gold in condoms and got it implanted in their small intestines by a special surgical procedure. Deputy Commissioner of the Intelligence Bureau was also present at the airport during the operation. Two inspectors, besides the superintendent of customs department, were also present at the time of the arrest.

83. 'Language' a barrier in filling PU seats

Patna: Urdu: 7/15, Hindi: 10/35, Persian, Maithili, Sanskrit : 0/45, This is not the scorecard of some of the students. Rather, it reflects the number of students who took admission in the above language courses offered at BN College his year! The disturbing trend is seen all over Patna University college campuses, where students are displaying a complete lack of interest in language honours courses. No wonder, the teachers are worried. For without students, there can be no classes. The trend is no better in other universities of Bihar.

"With just a couple of days left before the closing of admission, courses like Persian, Maithili and Sanskrit have failed to attract any students. Even Hindi, which used to be heavily opted for, has found very few takers this year," In language, only the English honours course has any takers. But, that doesn't mean that they wanted to learn it. "Many students taking admission

I believe that laughter is a language of God and that we can all live happily ever laughter – *Yakov Smirnoff.*

to BA English do not even know how to write one sentence in English without spelling or grammar mistakes! They are here just because a degree in English looks good." Patna College has a similar tale to tell. There are absolutely no takers for courses like Bengali, Arabic, Maithili, Sanskrit and Persian. The only streams that have garnered good responses in both the colleges are philosophy, sociology, political science, psychology, history, economics and geography. The biggest hits are the vocational courses, as they claim to offer better career prospects.

84. Dalit boy shot dead for refusing to clean plates

An 11-year-old Dalit boy was allegedly shot dead for refusing to clean plates at the dhaba he worked at, in Shamli district of Uttar Pradesh. District Police officials said the accused in the case has been identified as Jagpal Pandit, a resident of the area, who is on the run. He pulled out his gun and shot the victim in the stomach. Though this is a matter of investigation, the accused also used discriminatory language. The victim was rushed to the nearest hospital but was declared "brought dead on arrival," said the officer. His parents frequently told him he was the only child they could afford to send to school. The only indulgence he was watching television at a roadside dhaba near his hut.

85. Indian Lungs 30% weaker than Europeans'

New Delhi: In another proof that worsening air quality in Indian cities is affecting people's health, a study has found that Indians have 30% lower lung function as compared to Europeans. Things could get worse if immediate steps are not taken to curb vehicular emission, doctors warned. The study was conducted on 10,000 healthy, non-smoking individuals

---

I force myself to laugh at everything for fear of being obliged to weep
– Pierre-Augustin De Beaumarchais.

---

in Jaipur, Patna, Hyderabad, Kolkata and Kashmir. "We measured the Peak Ex-piratory Flow Rate (PEFR), the rate at which a person exhales, to assess lung function. North Indians but overall the results were appalling - was 30% lower than Europeans," said Dr. Sundeep Salvi, Director of Pune-based Chest Research Foundation. Who led the study.

86. Ninety per cent (90%) teachers fail skill and eligibility test

New Delhi : Two days ahead of Teacher's day the results of the Central Teacher's Eligibility Test (CTET) unveiled worrying picture: almost 90% of aspiring school teachers do not possess the requisite skills. The competency and skill test conducted by the CBSE shows that of the 776 lakh people who had appeared for the exam on July 28, 2013 only 77,354 could qualify the exam. The eligibility certificate is given to only those who secure 60% and above marks. Incidentally only around 1% of the aspirants could pass the exam held last year. A maximum of two tests can be held in a year. In 2012 two tests were held. There are two objective papers for CTET paper; 1 for those who were interested in becoming a teacher for class I to V and paper 2 for those desiring to be a teacher for class VI to VIII. Of the 2, 86,537 candidates who appeared for paper 1, only 33,184 qualified (11.58%). Of the 1,836,146 women who appeared in paper 1, only 12.19% could pass.

87. Chinese mom busted for breastfeeding on two-wheeler

Beljing: Meals on Wheels! A mom in China has been busted breastfeeding her baby as she rode a moped through busy roads, media reports said. The 18-month-old boy was reportedly

I like someone with a really good and dark sense of humour *- Paloma Faith.*
No one is more profoundly sad as one who laughs' too much *- Jean Paul.*

clinging on with his hands and lips as his mother weaved her way through busy traffic in Henan Province. The child was reportedly crying and the mother responded by taking one hand off the bike to get ready to breastfeed. The impromptu meal earned the woman a ticking off from the police, who threatened to confiscate the moped if she repeated the act.

88. New Law

Perhaps, it will stun you. In Bihar, a music teacher is less paid than a NREGA worker. Music teachers in Bihar colleges are required to work from 9 am to 4 pm every day for a meager salary of ₹3,000 per month. They may have to perform at other college activities, when required. But this is the reality that a music teacher came across when he applied for job in a top women's college of the state capital. He was stunned to find that the salary was too less for a qualified teacher. "Isn't it too less? I had expected better salary in the college," he said. "That is precisely what we want to know from you. Will you be able to work on this salary? We know it is too low for anybody to expect," the head of the institution told the applicant. The aspirant then asked as to why remuneration was not being increased, as college teachers draw decent salary. Well this is because candidates apply against vacancies. If you have a job elsewhere, join it said the college authority.

89. School of Thought

Former DGP DN Gautam is known for being candid and direct in his observations. The other day while talking about the right to education, he said had he been born today and studied in a village, he would not have become anything other than a NREGA worker. He was referring to the pitiable condition of

---

I like the laughter that opens the lips and the heart, that shows at the same time pearls and the soul – *Victor Hugo.*

---

school education in Bihar. "Perhaps, whatever the government does not want to do, it makes a law for it. Even when I was a kid, the schools in villages were much better than what they are today," he said.

90. Bangala govt. to take legal action against Nobel laureate

The Bangladesh government decided to take legal action against Nobel laureate Muhammad Yunus, who revolutionized the country's microcredit sector, for allegedly claiming tax exemption for his income from foreign sources.

A decision to this effect was taken at a cabinet meeting after the government received a report from the National Board of Revenue (NBR) following its investigation into Yunus' incomes from overseas sources since August 21, 2012.

The NBR report came a year after Prime Minister Sheikh Hasina ordered for a fresh probe into Yunus's activities and financial transactions in his later years as the Grameen Bank's managing director.

91. Spy games: ISI men caught cheating in Pakistan exam

Islamabad: Fifty Inter-Services Intelligence, better known as ISI, and intelligence bureau officials were among 500 candidates caught browsing internet on their phones to answer a recruitment exam for Pakistan's premier counter-terrorism agency. The exam was "marred by so many blatant frauds that it has turned into a farce." Question papers were not only distributed one-and-a-half hours after the start time, but were also not enough. Many examinees had to wait

***I live a very joyful life, with a lot of laughter and good times** – *Kimberly Elise.*

No religion has accepted the sense of humour as a quality.

longer, for the photo copies of the question paper. While most of the question papers multiple-choice, there were a few that required the aspirants to write a couple of paragraphs on ways to eradicate terrorism. "As the exam started, there were around 10 invigilators for 5,000 candidates, hundred of them busy cheating since they were allowed to bring mobile phones." Intelligence agency officials turned out to be the trouble makers as they started arguing with the invigilators when efforts were made to take away their phones. Candidates found cheating had been disqualified, the exam coordinator said.

92. Tata Tele scraps attendance to motivate staff

New Delhi: The boss wants to know what you did. Not where you are.

Do you really need to show up in office every day on time to deliver on your work expectation? Maybe not, if the example of Tata Teleservices Ltd (TTSL) is anything to go by. Moving towards a new age talent management system the telecom company done away with the habit of staff members marking their attendance. The company now does not have a daily time sheet, card swipe of turnstiles to monitor staff attendance. Instead, they are evaluated on their performance. "We have taken a liberal view on the working time of an employee," said executive president, human resources, TTSL. "The benefit for employees is that they can focus on their work rather than fret over their attendance. Apart from this, we provide opportunities to work from home depending upon the need of an employee." It is still not a entirely free hand for the staff, though, there is a sort of oblique attendance system, as the company records the time an employee spends on its network, from logging in to logging out.

I refuse not to have a sense of humour – *Kenneth Robert Livingstone.*
My whole effort here is to make you light, non-serious, laughing.

93. Kerala event that left Ansari embarrassed: Host notes VP was born on Fool's Day

Thiruvananthapuram: The Sree Narayana Dharma Samithi hosted a function to honour Shashi Tharoor, it turned out a disaster in protocol and etiquette. To say the least.

First, the compere prominent TV Show host and quiz master GS Pradeep, gave exaggerated and unnecessarily long-winded introductions of guests as he invited them to speak. Then, he made an uncalled for observation that Hamid Ansari, who presented the award to the union minister, was born on Fool's Day, much to the Vice President's embarrassment. And though he was born on April 1, Pradeep continued, Ansari was an intellectual. A few sentences later, he repeated the reference to the Vice President's birthday. And just when many thought Pradeep had caused enough embarrassment, a director of the Samithi got up to sing the national anthem. It was awful, for want of a milder word. Vijaya Prasad's rendition was out of tune, without clarity, full of mistakes in the lyrics, and he lost count of the repetitive ***"jaya he"*** towards the end. Ansari clearly wasn't amused: his office later inquired with Kerala Chief Protocol Officer K B Santhosh Kumar about the messy conduct of the event.

94. A pat For Azad

Health minister Ghulam Nabi Azad seems to have got a fan in WHO director general Margaret Chan who certified him as "one of the best" health minister in the world at the AIIMS convocation . At the inaugural programme of the south east Asia regional meet two days ago, she had praised Azad adding: " he hasn't paid me to say this."

I think laughter is sacred act – *Tom Shadyac*

No one is more profoundly sad than he who laughs too much – *Richter.*

---

95. Nainital HC order fails to curb animal sacrifices

Dehradun : More than 200 goats and sheep were sacrificed in Nainital disregarding the Nainital high court judgment of December 2011 that forbids animal sacrifice in Uttarakhand temples and protests of animal activists. Activists have in fact alleged that the local administration colluded with devotees in killing animals. The High Court had in its order clearly said that slaughtering of animals for other than human consumption was illegal.

96. Where human and snakes coȩxist peacefully

Vedaranyam (T.N.): In the shade of a grove is a stone structure of Veeran, the guardian deity of the hutments of velliammal and her three sons. Modestly decorated with specks of vermilion, the deity is seated a stone's throw from the Velliammal hutments a cluster of three huts and the Paambu Kulam (Snake pond) that fringes her backyard. The pond has been in existence for close to 28 years, she says.

In these times of human animal conflict, the pond in Marudhur village, some 20 km. from Vedaranyam, represents a tale of ecological harmony and coexistence between humans and the snakes that frequent their houses. Each year, the family of farm-wage labourers spends some money to desilt and deepen the pond so that the snakes can come and quench their thirst. Velliammal believes that the snakes guard not just Veeran but also her property. Her anecdotal references attest to her belief. "the household objects may lie around, and on several occasion, a snake will be guarding my property. No outsider can cross over or touch the objects, "she says. With the presence of peacocks in the fields posing a threat, the snakes are pushed

---

I think one reason for a successful marriage is laughter. I think laughter gets you through the rough moments in a marriage – Bob Newhart.

to human habitations, says Rani, Velliammal's daughter-in law. When the pond is dry, the women pump just enough water into it from the lift pump for the snakes to drink from.

97. Frequent errors

About 10 days after the land Bill was passed by Parliament, it was finally sent to President Pranab Mukherjee for his assent. The delay, it seems, was casued after several typographical and other errors were spotted in the Hindi draft of the Bill, which had to be rectified. Such mistakes are becoming quite frequent. Law minister Kapil Sibal had to apologize to Rajya Sabha during the Winter session for the government's failure to get a Constitution (amendment) Bill passed by Lok Sabha due to an error in the title of the Bill.

98. Recall coins with goddess image, petitioner tells court

Arguing that the depiction of the image of ***Mata Vaishno Devi*** on the new series of ₹5 and ₹10 coins would "hurt religious sentiments" as the state would be seen to be "espousing the cause of a single religion", a petition has been filed before the Delhi High Court to recall the new coins and prohibit circulation of the series.

According to the PIL filed through advocate Sachin Mishra, the coins which were released by the Reserve Bank of India in August, 2013 to commemorate the silver jubilee of the Mata Vaishno Devi Shrine Board. The plea contented that these coins would be "used everywhere including places such as liquor shops, meat shops, toilets, etc.", which would amount to a disrespect of the deity. The High Court declined to issue any orders on the plea and asked the petitioner to approach the

I think the most attractive thing is a sense of humour. If someone can make you laugh, you've gotten a lot out of the way – *Kiefer Sutherland.*

RBI with a modified representations seeking discontinuation of the series instead of a recall of the coins.

99. In the hamlets of Datia, a mystery bank for poor

Dariyavpur (Datia): Need a hassle-free loan? "***Lath maar bank***" might just be the ticket for you. Visit any of a dozen of villages deep inside Madhya Pradesh's Datia district – but on specific days – and wait in the morning for the gong to sound. The mystery "bank" which has been helping poor farmers for over 50 years, has no office. Its representatives - middle aged men all – visit the villages once a month on motorcycles. And their identity card? Red books with noting in Urdu. "Nobody knows who they are, nor do we ask," said Raghuveer a resident of Dariyavpur village, where they come on the 14th of every month. We call them the Lucknow wale sahukaar (lenders from Lucknow) as they are originally from Lucknow. Earlier, they used to carry lathis (sticks) so the bank came to be known as ***lath maar bank.*** What has endeared the lenders to the farmers is their humane approach - no documents, no mortgages, and no pressure to return money. Though the interest charged is 30% - exorbitant by the standards of regular banks – a person unable to repay the loan is merely blacklisted "All they require is a guarantor." Said Dariyavpur sarpanch Hukum Dev. The ***"Lath maar bank"*** lend money to those whom nobody helps," added kallu, a villager.

100. Ninety per cent (90%) of my colleagues uneducated, an embarrassment: Censor chief

Central Board of Film Certification (CBFC) chairperson Leela Samoson has claimed that 90 per cent of the panel members clearing movies in India are "uneducated" and an "embarrassment". "They can neither read nor write, cannot

I think there is nothing sexier than laughter lines – *Isla Fisher*
Nobody ever died of laughter – *Max Beerbohm.*

sign on the forms, leave alone read the script of the film they are watching or understand the responsibility that this empanelment entails," she said.

101. Man shot for omitting onion from omelet

Aligarh (UP): The lord of the rings is missing and there is chaos all around. In Uttar Pradesh's Etah district, a man shot a roadside vendor when the omelette he ordered was served minus onion. Elsewhere, a shopkeeper was thrashed when he served his customers chaat with radish instead of onions.

102. Dhoni lets his hair down, youth in Ranchi pick it up

Ranchi: Barely a day after he sported a new hairdo, youngsters in Ranchi, the Indian cricket captain's home town, have started becoming Mahendra Singh Dhoni lookalikes. Salons and men's beauty parlour received enquiries, and clients even demanded the new 'Dhoni hairstyle.' Former Pakistan President Pervez Musharraf once liked Dhoni's long locks and advised him to keep the hairdo as it suited his personality.

103. Five- year-old (5) booked in Arwal for 'breach of peace'

Patna: Onlookers present in the court of the sub-divisional magistrate (SDM) of Arwal in south-central Bihar were stunned when a five -year -old boy reached there to sign a bond in a criminal matter.

Perched on the shoulders of his father, the child was there as he had been booked under section 107 of the criminal procedure code (CrPC) in the aftermath of a case of arson in which a shop run by his uncle was set on fire. The child had to return home without signing the bond as the sub-divisional magistrate (SDM) did not hold court as he was called away for a meeting convened by the Arwal district magistrate. Top officials confirmed the incident. When confronted with the gravity of what had happened almost all of them were found looking for a place to hide?

Arwal superintendent of police Anand Kumar said the investigating officer (IO) of the case, Umeshwar Paswan, had been placed under suspension and departmental proceedings were being initiated against him.

DIG (Magadh range) Bachchu Singh Meena said he had directed inspectors and SDPs to henceforth mention the age of the accused in FIRs and physically verify the same.

104. Bihar woman 'jails' hubby for 9 years, draws his pension

Ara: Just how cruel can one's family be? A new benchmark in spousal torture has been set by a pitiless woman at Deuwar village under Sandesh police station in Bhojpur district of south central Bihar. Dhankeshri Devi, 50, it has now been revealed, kept her husband in confinement for nine years, got him declared dead and availed his pension for this entire period.

'In course of investigation, it will become clear how the mother son duo procured the forged death certificate. It will also be probed as to why neighbours kept mum for so long though they knew of Jagat's confinement, the SP told HT. The SHO said Jagat was quite disoriented when he was released from his prolonged confinement. "He kept on chanting 'Dumka. Dumka' a reference to the place where he was posted as peon till 2004." he added.

If it is medicine you are after, prescribe yourself some laughter.
Nothing is sillier than silly laughter – *Catullus.*

105. Life term convict earns an MU doctorate

Gaya: A lifetime convict of a murder case lodged for over 12 years in Gaya central jail, toiled day and night to finally earn a doctorate awarded by the Magadh University (MU), Bodh Gaya. Soon after receiving the MU notification regarding award of Ph.D. degree to Mohammad Sajjad Alam, who had appeared in viva voce exam held in MU on August 29, 2013 under heavy police custody, IG (prisons) Anand Kishore on Wednesday (9.10.2013) extended his congratulations to the convict-scholar through director probationer O.P. Gupta at Gaya prison. The news that – Qaidi number 7051- A became a 'Doctor' – surprised even the prison officials and other inmates. With a post-graduate degree in Urdu, he registered for Ph.D. in MU under the supervision of Dr Muhammad Mazhar Hussain, retired Principal of S.N. Sinha College, Jehanabad, on the topic Qurrat-Ul-Ain Hyder as a short story writer".

106. Pakistan temple to celebrate Durga puja

Kolkata: The first community organized Durga puja in Pakistan will be held at a 150-year old temple (Swami Narayan Mandir) on a road named after Pakistan's founder M.A. Jinnah in Karachi.

At the Puja, the Sanskrit Shlokas chanted will be written in Urdu script sine the Hindus in Pakistan are not proficient in Sanskrit or Hindi. "The Gita, written in the Urdu script, is available in cities such as Lahore."

107. Sacrificial animals in Pak costlier than a car this Eid

Islamabad: With preparations for Eid -ul-Zoha in full swing across Pakistan, a scramble for buying sacrificial animals at the

If love is the treasure, laughter is the key – *Yakov Smirnoff.*
People come in walking laughing and talking.

last minute has begun. Yet, much to the chagrin of the general public, several animal have reportedly also been stolen from homes.

This year, the average price of a "qurbani" or a sacrificial animal begins from 20,000 Pakistani rupees and goes up to a princely sum of ₹16 Lakh – an amount that has left several appalled, considering a brand new car in Pakistan costs only about ₹7 lakh.

108. Lankan sailor who hit Rajiv is now astrologer, music seller

Colombo: About 7 km. from Colombo's Fort area on the second floor of the Nugegoda supermarket, sits a bearded, bespectacled and balding man, with two computers on his desk and shelves with music CDs and cassettes. There is nothing really remarkable about the shop which sells music and some stationery products. Except its 46-year- old astrologer-owner. In 1987, Vijitha Rohana Wijemuni was a Sri Lankan Navy sailor. And on July 30 that year he tried to hit the then Indian Prime Minister Rajiv Gandhi with his rifle butt during a guard of honour at the Sri Lankan President's House in Colombo. He had swung his rifle. But Rajiv managed to duck and miss the full brunt of the blow, even though the rifle struck him. Wijemuni was quickly restrained, court-martialed and jailed for six years. He was let off after about two- and- half years by President R. Premadasa through a presidential pardon.

He now sells CDs of Buddhist chants, some Sinhala movies and even old Hindi hits. He says he does not want to talk after this reporter is introduced as an Indian journalist. After some persuasion, he agrees to only talk about his astrology and nothing about the Rajiv incident.

If people can laugh more, the world will certainly be better.
Real happiness is not in the senses but above the senses – *Swami Vivekananda.*

---

109. When Ravan refused to die!

Patna: The phailin effect that brought in its wake strong gusts of winds and non-stop rains played a spoilsport during the ritual buring of Ravan effigy on October 13, 2013. The tall effigy of Ravan, especially built for the occasion, soggy after the rains, refused to burn this time on Dussehra! The effigy was then soaked with petrol and diesel but to no avail. However, Shree Dusehra Committee Trust organised the event ***"Ek Sham Prashasan Ke Naam"*** to felicitate government personnel based in Patna. 'for 24 x 7 duty'.

110. Bhopal wants 'park first, toilet later'

Bhopal: An early application of PM hopeful Narendra Modi's one-liner 'toilets first, temples later' has run a ground in a Bhopal park named after 16th century poet Goswami Tulsidas.

The Bhopal Municipal Corporation (BMC) has had to abandon toilet construction near the statue of Tulsidas who wrote the Ramcharitmanas in Tulsi Park following strong opposition from the people. However, workers had already dug up the small triangular park to lay the foundation. "The government has so much land. Why inside the Tulsi Park?" said Pawan Kumar, a resident. 'It is strange authorities allowed construction inside the park without considering that the park is meant for the local residents," he wondered. BMC engineers had a different take. "It is residents who have turned the park into a public urinal, "said BMC deputy chief engineer O.P. Bhardwaj on the phone.

111. Sikh denied bus ride for wearing kirpan

Los Angeles: A sikh student, in California was not allowed to board bus after the driver raised objection to his wearing

If you can laugh at it then you can live with it *– Unknown Source.*
Seven days without laughter makes one weak *– Mort Walker.*

a ceremonial knife or kirpan and called the police. Harsimran Singh, a student of University of California, said he has travelled for the last two years with kirpan and did not face any issues earlier.

112. Malaysian court rules use of 'Allah' exclusive to Muslims

Kuala Lumpur: In a landmark judgment, a Malaysian court ruled that non-Muslims cannot use the word "Allah" to refer to God and prohibited a Christian newspaper from using it in the Muslim-majority nation. "It is our common finding that the usage of the name 'Allah' is not an integral part of the faith and practice of Christianity," said Justice Apandi, who read out the summary of the judgment.

Hearald editor Father Lawrence Andrew, responding to the verdict, said the ruling was flawed and Church would appeal against the ruling.

113. Unemployed couple in China 'sells' daughter to buy iPhone

Bejing: A young unemployed Chinese couple, who allegedly sold their baby girl and used part of the money to buy an iPhone and other expensive items, are facing criminal charges, state media reported. Shanghai prosecutors have brought a case against the couple identified as Zheng and Teng for human trafficking after they put their third child up for adoption through illegal online postings and accepted money for the baby, the Liberation Daily reported.

The couple began posting online advertisements for the child. The advertisements suggested they would be willing to part

If you generate laughter you will be sought after. Serious is a sin, so learn to laugh. We don't laugh because we are happy, we are happy because we laugh - *William James.*

with their unborn baby in exchange for up to 50,000 yuan ($8,200). However, prosecutors said the couple's bank records clearly show they had hatched "sinister conspiracy" to profit from the child's sale.

114. Woman drops rape complaint: 'Grant him bail, so we can marry'

Tells court she made a mistake, judge says get married in a month.

New Delhi: A city court found itself caught in the minds of lover's spat, with a young woman pressing charges of rape after a fight and later asking for the man's bail so that she could marry him.

The court of Additional Sessions Judge Dharmesh Sharma granted bail, while directing them to get married within a month. "I committed a mistake in filing the complaint for which I am sorry. I am still in love and I wish to marry him. I request that he may be released on bail so that we can marry", the woman told ASJ Sharma. The bail was granted on a bond of ₹15,000 with "directions that on the next date of hearing, the proof of marriage be shown to the court".

115. Music in the air

New Delhi: The lunch hosted by Chinese Premier Li Kequiang for Prime Minister Manmohan Singh in Beijing had an interesting sidelight. The people's Liberation Army (PLA) band had put together a unique selection of Indian music for the visiting delegations that took many by surprise. The music started with the famous *Mera Naam Chin Chin Chu*. Bollywood number that was based on a dancer from Shanghai followed by A. R. Rahman number *Roja Janeman* and *Gore Gore Banke*

In groups, women laugh more than men. Women also laugh more at men more than men laugh at women.

chhorey. The final Indian number that took the case was *Baar Baar Dekho, Hazar Baar Dekho*. At the end of the meal, Singh went over and felicitated the Chinese band. Later, at a dinner by Chinese President Xi jinping too Bollywood numbers were played but the star attraction was a Bharatnatyam performance by three Chinese dancers.

116. Three hundred (300) Railway staff killed by trains every year, most of them while inspecting tracks

New Delhi: A railway employee dies in the line of duty on four days out of five, making his job statistically far more dangerous than that of security forces in some of India's most violent combat zones. An average 300 railway men have been killed in accidents every year over the past 4-5 years. Most of them were run over by trains as they patrolled the tracks to ensure there were no fractures in the rails. A major reason for derailments. A technological solution is needed.

117. Brazil doesn't have money to send its officials to India

New Delhi: India is not the sole emerging economy feeling the bite of the current financial situation and implementing a slew of measures to counter it. Brazil also facing a significant slowdown has decided to keep its pockets tight and refused to send a team of high-level officials to India for a bilateral meeting. "It was proposed to hold the India-Brazil joint working group (JWG) meeting in India and two set of dates were proposed by India in August 2013. However, the Brazilian side expressed inability to travel to India due to austerity measures prevailing in Brazil and decided to hold the meeting through video-conferencing," reads a petroleum ministry's note to the ministry of external affairs.

***In my mind, there is nothing so illiberal and so ill-bred as audible laughter** - Earl of Chestetfield.*

---

118. Small families threat for Hindus, have more kids

Kochi: For the Rashtriya Swayamsevak Sangh (RSS) it's the more the merrier.

On the lines of the Catholic church's campaign to have more children and win rewards, the RSS has advised Hindus to go for bigger families and not to limit their number of children. Concerned over the size of Hindu families, it has asked community members not to follow family planning norms blindly and create small families.

The sangh feels that big families will help check the menacing demographic changes taking place in many parts of the country. The one child norm practiced by most Hindu families will endanger the very existence of the community. It warned. "According to the 2011 census, growth rate of children in the age group of 0—6 is 15% among Hindus, whereas it is 18% among Muslims. Small family norms are posing a big threat to Hindus. So each family should have three children," Two years ago, a worried Catholic Church in Kerala had announced a mega-plan ***Jeeva Samrudhi*** - to encourage families with more than three children. It even coined the slogan of ***'big family happy family'***, and decided to bear educational and other expenses of families who have more than three children. According to the latest census report, Christian population has come down to 18.75% from the earlier 22% in the state, forcing the church to press the panic button.

119. Man penalized for leaving bag at airport

Patna: Leaving a bag is fraught with risk. Balwant, a local villager, realized it the hard way after he was penalized ₹200 for

In this life he laughs longest who laughs last – *John Masefield.*
One good, hearty laugh is a bombshell exploding i n a right place – *De Witt Talmage.*

troubling the airport security agencies here. Balwant had gone to see off a relative to the Jayaprakash Narayan International airport in the morning. It so happened that after his kin had entered the airport terminal building, Balwant left his bag and took a walk to quench his thirst. Not spotting a source of free potable water nearby, Balwant took a walk around the airport periphery to scout for one. It may have taken him 20 minutes to locate one and return to the canopy area where he had left his bag under a steel chair, but the intervening period was tense for airport security personnel.

120. Beware, Chor mama-bhanja on prowl in Purnia

Purnia : If you happen to live in Kasba, about 12 km. to the north from here, and your wish has been granted, it's time for you to play a thief. And giving company in observing the *chor vrat* (festival of theft) will be your *chor bhanja* (nephew). Weird it many sound, but keeping with the 500-year-old tradition people in Kasba town have been observing the *'chor vrat'* that begins on no moon day (Diwali) and concludes with Chhath-puja.

Speaking about the significance of the age-old tradition, Nirmal Jha, 50, a priest at Kasba, said the festival dispelled darkness from the life of people by leading them towards light. "That is why it starts from Amavasya (no moon day) and ends with Chhath-puja when devotes offered obeisance to Sun," he said. "All the people celebrating the festival take a pledge to follow a life free from sin. This collectiveness gives them power to fight evils unitedly," he added. Gautam Pandey 55, another priest, said the *chor vrat* was celebrated to dispel the ill mind which was "behind all crimes in the world and spread the light of divinity." During the festival, a person, whose wish had been fulfilled, takes the role of 'chor mama' who along with his 'chor

Instead of singing, laugh as take a shower.
That laughter can be healing is quite revealing.

bhanja' tries to steal things from someone's house. In case they are caught the women of the house trim their hairs.

"The festival is also entirely eco-friendly, A *'chor mama'* and his *'chor bhanja'* generally use wigs made of jutes. The use of chemical is strictly prohibited, Gangu pandit, 60, a resident of Kasba said. Trimming of the tresses signified cutting the sin of the *chor mama,*" he added.

121. Mahatma's *Charkha* fetches Pound 1,00,000 at auction in UK

London: Mahatma Gandhi's famous *Charkha* that he used in Yerwada jail during the Quit India movement fetched a whopping Pound 1,00,000 at the auction for historical documents and arte-facts by Mullock's Auction house in Shropshire. The auction house, however, refused to name the buyer.

Made of Indian teak, the *Charkha,* with a minimum bid of Pound 60,000 was used by Gandhi during his term at the Pune jail and was gifted to American Free Methodist missionary Revd Floyd A Puffer by him in 1935. Puffer was a pioneer in Indian educational and industrial cooperatives who invented the bamboo plow that was adopted by Gandhi. Puffer, along with his wife, worked as a missionary in India during the independence movement. In 1935 displayed Gandhi's spinning wheel at a number of talks and events.

Mullock's has put over 60 of Gandhi's prized possessions for auction, including important documents, photographs and books. The auction house's specialist Richard Westwood Brookes said, "The *Charkha* is one of Gandhi's most prized possessions as he devised the workings of it himself. It was

It is better to write of laughter than of tears, for laughter is the property of man – *Francois Rabelais.*

used by him in Yerwada Jail whilst fighting for the rights and independence of India. It has impeccable provenance and is unquestionably the most important Gandhi arte-fact we have ever sold. The *Charkha* was the physical embodiment and symbol of Mahatma Gandhi, he once said, "In my dream, in my sleep, while eating, I think of the spinning wheel. The spinning wheel is my sword. To me it is the symbol of India's liberty," Brookes said.

122. PRICELESS POSSESSIONS: 'Should refrain from putting price on Bapu's items'

New Delhi: If Mahatma Gandhi belongs to all humanity and not just India, it is also the responsibility of the citizens of the world to refrain from putting a price tag on his items, feels Tara Gandhi Bhattacharjee, granddaughter of Mahatma Gandhi.

"Gandhi was synonymous with ethical, spiritual and human values. How can we put a price tag on a value that is priceless? How can we auction a value?" Tara Gandhi vice-chairperson of Gandhi Smiriti, told HT. "Unfortunately Gandhi's item can be duplicated, multiplied and sold, brought and auctioned in a thoughtless way."

"Whenever Gandhi had an extra pencil, a pen, a walking stick or any other extra item, he would give away these possessions to various people from all over the world. Today Gandhi belongs to the entire humanity; his items are priceless for human heritage."

In fact, instead of auctioning, the best way to respect Gandhi's heritage is to create an education for children that lays emphasis on non-violence and compassion.

It is easier to make people cry than to make them laugh – *Unknown Source.*
Our sincerest laughter with some pain is fraught – *Percy Byshe Shelley.*

---

123. EC takes traditional route to lure voters

Barmer: The Barmer election department has taken the help of tradition to come up with an initiative to encourage people to vote. Distributing **'peela chawal'** or yellow rice, is an age-old custom in western Rajasthan to ensure attendance of the community at marriages and other social functions, Instead of invitation cards, this rice is sent to potential guests who, when they accept it, have a social obligation to attend an event. "Migrants (a big section of people in this region were migrants who live outside the area for their job or business) have not been returning to cast their vote, which is why at the last election, the voting percentage in many places was very low." "This time, when they came home for Diwali, was approached them and invited them for voting by giving them **"peela chawal." "Good use of tradition."**

124. De-stress in Indonesia with the new snake massage

Jakarta: Lying on a massage table at a spa in the Indonesian capital Jakarta, Feri Tilukay closed his eyes and smiled blissfully as three enormous snakes slithered all over him. He is one of a small band of customers brave enough to try the "snake massage", where the gentle hands of a professionally trained masseuse are swapped for the cold, scaly skin of 1.8 metre pythons. "It is unique sensation", Tilukay 31, said, as the snakes slid over him, adding the treatment "gives you an dreamline rush".

125. '1913 Nobel' menu to be replicated for VIPs

New Delhi: Hundred years after Rabindranath Tagore won the Nobel Prize for Literature, the embassy of Sweden in Delhi will host a VIP dinner to pay tribute to the Nobel laureate. The dinner will serve the menu of 1913 Nobel banquet – in which Tagore took part – to the guests. Tagore won the prize that year.

The dinner, part of the Sweden India Nobel Memorial Week 2013, will include senior representatives from the governments of both countries. "The responsible chief of the Nobel banquet, Mark Phoenix will travel to Delhi... as a tribute to Tagore, the menu from 1913 will be replicated. The whole menu from the Nobel gala dinner, both food and wine, will be the same. Except for the turtle soup, we are serving everything. The chef will try and retain the essence of the feast, which Tagore was part of after winning the Nobel Prize," Harald Sandberg, Ambassador of Sweden to India said. In 1913 menu included Tortue clarie, Supreme de turbotin Walewska, Poularde Massenet, Chaufroix de cailles Lucullus, Salade, Fondfs d'artchauts Maintenon, Parfait praline, Friansises and fruits. The wine served were Madere Old, Chateau Smith Haut Lafite, 1905, Rudesheimer, 1908, Charles Heidsieck, Brut, 1904 and Porto. Very Superior Old. According to him preparations for the dinner had started weeks back and ingredients had been sourced from across the country. The Nobel Memorial Wall with busts of Tagore will also be inaugurated at the Rajiv Chowk and HUDA City Centre metro stations.

126. Toilets double up as kitchens on trains, admits Railways

Thiruvananthapuram: Toilets can be good kitchens also, according to Indian Railways. In an affidavits, to a lok adalat in Kochi, the southern railway food commissioner admitted that some of the lavatories of the Thiruvananthapuram-Kanpur Jan

It is well known that Beauty does not look with a good grace on the timid advances of Humour – *W. Somerset Maugham.*

Shatabdi had indeed been converted into mini kitchens. The lok adalat was hearing a petition seeking better hygiene and quality food in pantries of long-distance trains. Cockroaches and bugs routinely find their way into rail meals. Though the railways claims the mini kitchens are equipped with water purifiers, zinc wash basins, coolers and mini fridge, none of them exist in a majority of trains. The commissioner reasoned out that the toilets were properly cleaned and disinfected before being converted into kitchens.

127. Matrimony route to fake currency racket

Purnia: In Seemanchal region where the 'syndicate' operating the fake currency rackets, recruits poor youths after getting them married off in the neighbouring states West Bengal & Bihar and vice versa.

Marriage helps such people establish rapport with the locals, later; they carry out the racket with ease without being suspected. This came to the light during the recent raids at various places in the Seemanchal region, carried out by West Bengal police in the aftermath of Tunda's arrest.

128. Flying pilotless: Air India audit discovers 400 ghost staff on rolls

New Delhi: Some 400 employees of Air India (AI) have been "missing" from work, some of them for as long as seven years. The missing employees include around 50 pilots and 200 cabin crew, the rest belong to the engineering and other departments.

Top human resources officials at AI made the baffling discovery during an internal check last month. The missing employees

Unless your belly goes into ripples you are not laughing. People laugh from the head; they should laugh from the belly.

have not drawn salaries for the time they have been absent – some of them since 2006 – but they have not been struck off the rolls either. Notices have been sent to the missing employees. "No one has any clue about these employees. They may have joined another airline, or may be doing something else". The HR audit also found that 17 employees, who are office-bearers of various unions at the airline, had not been reporting for duty but continued to draw salaries. "We have to provide office space, telephone connections and a little bit of freedom in terms of office timings to office-bearers of employee unions. AI's over 13,000 employees are represented by 15 recognised unions.

129. Take the goat and savour the win!

Purnia: A victory in a sporting event is always followed by party. Aware of this fact, organisers of a village-level volleyball tournament in Purnia district decided to give away 'khassi' (goats) to winners and runners-up so that they could enjoy a feast of sumptuous mutton delicacies after the event. The move did sharp criticism from some animal protection groups, but the organisers claimed it was well-intentioned initiative to popularise games and sports in rural areas. The goats – weighing 20 kg to the winners representing Matiyapur and 15 kg to the runners-up from Sarsoni – were given as prizes after the final match of volleyball tournament at Kankhudia village in Jalalgarh police station area of the district. The tournament which drew a large number of spectators, was organised at the initiative of district board member Bibi Najma.

"In fact the number of teams interested in taking part of the meet swelled the moment we announced that goats would be given away as prizes instead of trophies. Finally, we selected six teams to play in the tournament," a member of the organising

Seriousness has become almost part of our bones and blood. Seriousness is a sin, and it is a disease.

committee said. "The event was a huge success and we somewhat succeeded in reviving sporting activity in the rural areas," Mohammad Sayeed, husband of Najma said.

130. Six EC official trek 5 km. to ensure two people can vote

Raipur: During the second phase of Chhatisgarh polling on November 19, 2013 a makeshift centre will be set up for two voters inside the forested zone of Seradand, about 350 km. north of Raipur. A six-member polling staff will trek through difficult terrain for over 5 km. after covering 15 km. of dirt track on tractor to carry an electronic voting machine (EVM) to the spot in north Koriya district to enable two tribals (a sect of Gond) – father Devraj (56) and son (19) – exercise their right to franchise. Phoolmatia (49) died of snake bite in August, 2013. This is the only two-voter polling centre in the country.

131. Tonk's serial candidate an octogenarian Maulana

Jaipur: Eighty-six year-old Maulana Wajid Ali has made a record of sorts. Since 1970, he has been standing for elections – but hasn't won a single one to date. Panchayats, blocks, assembly – this farmer from Tonk is not particular about office. Ask him about the number of nominations he has filed, and he is at a loss. After all, it has been 43 years since he started. The hobby, though, is a tad expensive. The security deposit now is ₹10,000 – and he has lost it every time. But no one minds, not even the locals who pool in the money. "My father never gets more than 70 votes. I do not remember him ever winning," says Ali's son Nahid. And Ali has no intention of giving up. "I might have missed the chance this time but I'll keep contesting till I die."

132. Bihar's 'sparrow man' and his winged 'friends'

Patna: Arjun Singh, 48, lost his father and wife in quick succession in 2004 and 2005. Then followed a long spell of depression and "utter lonliness", until in 2007 a fledging that had fallen from a tree in the courtyard of his house transformed his life for good.

He tended to the bird for a few days. It recovered and flew off, kicking off a passionate association with sparrows. Today (21.11.2013), about 8,000 birds of this fast disappearing species live in and around his sprawling ancestral home in Neraipur village of Rohtas district, about 170 km. south east of Patna. At his call, *aao aao* (come, come) the birds descended from skies and eat the grains he offers them every day. It has been estimated that every year he feeds at least six quintals of rice grains to the birds. "When I sit down for lunch, these lovely birds gather around me and try to pick food from my plate. When I walk around in my house they don't fly away, but just step aside and keep chirping. They have accepted me as their own. They have removed my loneliness," said Singh, a post-graduate in chemistry.

133. Fourteen-year-old's (14) 546-run knock sends records tumbling

Mumbai: Enter Prithvi Shaw, 14, standing at just over the five feet, he stood tall at Azad Maidan, the ground where Mumbai cricketer dreams are built. Playing for Rizvi Springfield (Bandra), he struck a mammoth 546 in a Harris Shield (Elite division) match against St. Francis D'Assisi. Displaying astonishing stamina, Prithvi, who started batting on Tuesday (November 19, 2013) lasted six hours and seven minutes. His 330-ball knock was

Laugh at yourself.....not others. If you laughed at yourself, then others' laughter towards you won't disturb you. You will feel happy.

laced with 85 fours and five sixes (an astounding strike rate of 165.45). His team was finally all out for 691. The innings is the third highest ever, after AEJ Collins' 628 (not out) in 1899 and CJ Eady's 566 at Hobart in 1901. It was the highest score in the 117 year-old tournament. He also became India's highest scorer. Prithvi took to cricket aged four. His father Pankaj Shaw even moved from Virar to Santa Cruz to ease his son's burden of commuting. And Prithvi is already soaring high.

134. Thief falls into pit, police have to help him out

New Delhi: This 16-year old boy's troubles began when he set out to rob a medical store at 2 am. It ended with him falling into a pit, screaming for help and, eventually, the police pulling him out to save his life.

Raman Goel, owner of the medical store, said the guard in the market called him around 3 am, saying a thief had entered his shop. "He told me the thief had broken open the shutter and the glass of the store. I told him to gather the locals till I reached here," he said. Goel, the resident and police began to search the shop and the basement. Just as they were wondering how the thief had managed to escape, they heard a cry for help, ***"Bachao, Bachao."*** It was coming from a pit that Goel had dug in his basement to drain out rain water. "We rushed to the pit and saw a person stuck horizontally in the pit. We could see his leg and back. It was the thief we had been looking for," Goel said.

The next two hours were taken up in rescue operation. "We had to dig around the pit to widen it and pull the boy out. It took a lot of effort, but we managed to pull him out," Goel said.

The juvenile was quick to thank his rescuers, police said. He was given a glass of water and sent to a juvenile home.

Mobile phone laughter during the day – when you are in a formal situation or waiting, just place your mobile on your ear and start talking to a friend pretending that he/she is telling you a joke.

135. In Bihar, every fourth primary, middle teacher failed Class V-level test

Patna: In September, 2013, 43,477 primary and middle school contractual teachers recruited by the Bihar government took the mandatory **"competency test"**, which is based on the syllabi of classes 3-5. Of these 10,614 teachers, or about 24 per cent, failed the test. The state government has recruited over 2.5 lakh contractual teachers since it launched its mega drive to fill the vacancies in 2007. These teachers get two chances to clear the "**competency test**" in the course of their service. The test has objective questions in English, Mathematics, Science, Hindi and General Knowledge, with no negative marking. The pass mark is 45 per cent for teachers belonging to general category and 40 per cent for the rest. If a teacher fails the test in both attempts, he loses his job. While middle school teachers must be graduates, primary school teachers must have passed their Class 12 exam. "We have been conducting **'competency test'** since 2009. Most questions are taken from classes 3, 4 and 5, only a few questions are of matriculation level." said State Council of Education Research and Training (SCERT) director Hasan Waris, adding the question paper models were duly advertised.

136. Khakis gone, cops remain 'casteists'

Patna: When they are in uniform and on duty they are constables of Bihar Police responsible for protecting the life and liberty of people, irrespective of caste, creed or community. But when they are in their own backyard in the barracks and the uniform is back on the rack, the Yadavs, Bhumiars, Brahmins, Paswans, Rajputs, Muslims in them come screaming to the fore. So much so, that they live and sleep in areas segregated on the

---

No man who has once heartily and wholly laughed can be altogether irreclaimably bad *– Thomas Carlyle.*

---

basis of caste and community and eat from kitchens earmarked on the same lines. And god forbids that somebody advises to the contrary, the state notwithstanding. Just imagine the Indian Army practicing untouchability. The country would have long lost its independence.

137. AIIMS-P applicants shock all

Patna: When officials at the All India Institute of Medical Sciences, Patna (AIIMS-P) decided to advertise posts for junior residents and teachers on July 26, 2013, little would have known, that they would be hit by a deluge of another kind, and that would shock them proper.

It did. For 90% who did apply for various posts were non-doctors and persons not at all fit for any of the posts advertised. Many did not have even the mandatory basic MBBS degree. Officials said, 44 non-MBBS degree holders, including those with degrees in technology, pharmaceuticals, computer applications, engineering and science, and even people with only school-level qualifications had applied for the position of teacher at the medical institute. "The bachelor of medicine and bachelor of surgery (MBBS) is the basic professional degree awarded on graduation from a medical school. It was unusual and unique, that scores of unqualified youth applied for teaching posts, including that of senior and junior residents at AIIMS-Patna," AIIMS-Patna director GK Singh said.

Anuj Kumar Kamal, with a degree in commerce and Sohan Lal Sonu, an arts graduate thought themselves supremely fit to be teachers of medicine and applied for the post of junior resident at AIIMS-Patna. If they could, why couldn't Amit Kumar Shrivastav apply having as he did, a bachelor of science degree in agriculture! Shrivastav also applied to be senior resident at

Nothing shows a man's character more than what he laughs at.
She laughs at everything you say. Why? Because she has fine teeth.

AIIMS-Patna. Rahul Bhardwaj, who has not finished graduation, sought to be considered for the same post while Bachcha Kumar Rajak, who holds a masters in commerce degree but applied for the post of senior resident at AIIMS-Patna. Dr. Singh said all such applicants had been rejected.

138. PMO tweet misspells name of Japanese empress

New Delhi: The government faced some embarrassing moments soon after the Japanese royal couple landed here on Saturday (30.11.2013) evening. Even as the Prime Minister and his wife went to receive emperor and empress Michiko at the airport, his twitter handle misspelt the name of the empress as Kimicho. The mistake was spotted within minutes and went viral on the social media. The tweet was soon deleted by the PMO but not before the Japanese embassy noticed the error. Japanese officials said this was an important symbolic visit and should treat with care. PM's communications advisor, Pankaj Pachauri said: "It was a typographical error which was corrected immediately."

139. Patil returned 155 gifts she received as President

New Delhi: Former President Pratibha Patil has returned 155 gifts that she had received during her tenure that were loaned to an NGO called Vidya Bharati Shaikshanik Mandal, Amravati, for display. The gifts include a stone box gifted by the US President, a candle-set from 10 Downing Street, a marble memento to embellished with pure gold leaf gifted during a regional anti-corruption meet in Delhi and several silver mementoes. They were returned in May, 2013.

Laugh, and the whole world laughs with you; weep and, you will weep alone.
Laugh like a drain *– laugh very loudly.* ***Laugh if you are wise*** *– Martial.*

A policy decision has been taken to henceforth display all gifts received during the tenures of various Presidents in the Rashtrapati Bhavan Museum.

140. Abducted girl offered herself as hostage to save schoolmates

Guwahati: Gunjan Sharma, one of the 11 children abducted in a school van in Assam's Simaluguri town, pleaded with the gunman to take her alone hostage and let the others go, revealed one of the 10 little children who escaped. Gunjan herself was found early morning near Bihubhor, near the Nagaland border, where the gunman freed her. Chief Minister Tarun Gogoi has announced an award of ₹2 lakh to Gunjan, who has since returned home.

141. Bihar panchayat decree: Pay down to marry rapist!

Katihar: A village panchayat in Katihar district of eastern Bihar has directed the father of a rape victim to pay dowry to the rapist's family so that she could get married to the accused boy! The diktat was issued a week ago but the matter came to light when the 16-year-old victim, along with her father, took up the matter with Katihar SP Asgar Imam at his janta darbar.

In villages of this area, custom often hold sway over law of the land. The victim said a boy from her neighborhood had raped while she was picking wood in a nearby field.

142. Jurisdiction of humour

Every now and then judges remind us that they too have a funny bone. The fact that humour can find its way into even the official proceedings of a court can perhaps be held the beginning of its ultimate conquest.

Laugh, and the whole world laughs with you; Weep, and you weep alone.
Yes, artificially indu ced laughter has the same medical benefits as natural laughter.

So, last month (November, 2013), a man approached the court challenging his arrest, ostensibly made to prevent his committing a crime in the foreseeable future. The police had a watertight case against the man, the most striking evidence being that he was drinking tea in a **'suspicious'** manner. And there was no 'satisfactory explanation' for this action. In a rare instance of delicate sarcasm in court judgements, the order read: "We were unaware that the law required anyone to give an explanation for having tea, whether in the morning, noon or night. One may take tea in a variety of ways, not all them elegant or delicate, some of them perhaps even noisy. But we know of no way to drink tea **'suspiciously'**".

143. Executives turn down jobs that cut into weekends

Weekends at work may soon be a thing of the past, say staffing experts, claiming that Indian managerial-level employees are rejecting job offers from companies that operate six days a week. According to Executive Access, an executive search firm, about 50% candidates ask for a job that offers them a five-day work week. Five to seven years ago, this number was at 20%. The data cuts across industries and clearly points to how employees are taking charge of their lives by setting aside more time for personal matters.

With candidates themselves becoming more vocal about the need for a proper work-life balance. Randstad India says over the last couple of years, they have seen a noticeable shift in employees' working patterns. "Today, the work-place mantra is "work smart, not long." Staying late in office and putting in long hours is not the sign of a workaholic anymore; it demonstrates inefficiencies caused by increasing workload." said Moorthy K. Uppalpuri, CEO, Randstad India.

Laugh, enjoy yourself, be more and more light.
Present mirth has present laughter.

---

144. Nursing homes booked for delivery on 11-12-13

Patna: Whether it is auspicious or just a unique date to remember, not only couples are choosing 11-12-13 to the nuptial knot, but the expectant mothers too have approached various nursing homes in the city to go for a C-section to deliver their baby. This sequential pattern of 11-12-13 has come after a century. "My daughter-in-law is in her full-term is supposed to deliver in the next few days. But we have already settled for a caesarean on 11-12-13, as we believe that it will bring good luck to the family." said Sarita Sahay, a resident of Boring Canal Road.

Dr. N.K. Lal, owner of a popular nursing home in Patliputra Colony area said, "Yes, we also had enquiries for C-sections on 11-12-13. In fact, we had to turn down the request for a woman, who was only in the eight month of her pregnancy," Gynaecologist Dr. S.L. Srivastava said she too had cases to handle on December 11, 2013. "But, incidentally, one of them went into labour before the scheduled date and the expectant mother's plan did not materialise," she said. "Ironic dates have become a trend. Over 500 couples tied the knot on 12-12-12. The same is going to happen on 11-12-13," said Ayesha Jha, a wedding planner.

145. Thieves in burqa open ATM vault, make off with ₹16 lakh

Mumbai: Two thieves dressed in burqa opened the vault of an ATM in Kalher on Bhiwandi Thane Road on Saturday (7.12.2013) night and made away with nearly ₹16 lakh. While there was only one CCTV camera installed in the kiosk, no security guard had been posted.

Laughing at oneself kills the ego and you are more transparent, more light, when you move in the world.

146. Paid with lashes for 3 kg. fish!

Katihar: Imagine a situation where a man paid to protect and guard you, suddenly turns against you! This is exactly what happened, when a policeman not only beat up a man but also confined him illegally, because he dared to charge ₹600 – the price of 3 kg fish from a station house officer here! Md. Shabbir (25), a resident of Salehpur under Falka police station has complained to Katihar SP, accusing SHO Falka police station, Sanjay Das with beating him mercilessly, besides keeping him in illegal custody as he had just asked for payment of ₹600, the cost of 3 kg. fish, which he had taken from him ten days ago. "I was released on Wednesday (11.12.13) after my family members paid the SHO." Before releasing me he took my signature on a blank paper." He also alleged that ₹3562 was taken away from his pocket during his illegal detention." SP Asgar Imam said, "The police officer if found guilty would be brought to book. The law does not discriminate." SHO Sanjay Das said, he had no knowledge about the incident. "I have been suffering from cold for the last three days." "Can anyone eat fish when he has cold and cough?" he asked.

147. 'Love' knows no SC bar in Dumraon!

Dumraon: They are unfazed by the verdict of Supreme Court barring physical relations of transgender, bisexual, lesbians and gays in private. They swear by the name of Zila Singh of Station Road in Dumraon subdivision of Buxar district. Zila Singh, a retired mechanic of erstwhile Bihar State Electricity Board (BSEB), had married a boy Lali, creating furore in Dumraon. Poonam, an eunch, staying in Thateri Bazaar locality of Dumraon says, whatever might be the judgement of the Supreme Court, many from our community have love affair

---

Laughter and cheer with the smell of beer.
***The highest state is laughter** – Maharishi Mahesh Yogi.*

---

with boys of Dumraon. Many transgender here do not wish to come out and speak about their affairs with them. Poonam, who is also famous for her social work, says, "Many from our community know that our affairs with men won't last, but it is 'they' who fall for our 'beauty.' "This will continue in Dumraon as love is blind," she concluded.

148. Woman says husband raped and tortured her on honeymoon

New Delhi: Barely a few-days after her marriage, a 26-year-old woman has alleged that she was confined, brutally tortured and sodomised by her husband during their honeymoon in Thailand. The woman, a resident of Palam in Southwest Delhi, filed a complaint against her husband after she arrived in Delhi. In her complaint, the woman alleged that her husband sexually assaulted her on the very night of the honeymoon. He allegedly forced her to consume alcohol and slapped her when refused to comply. She also alleged that her husband took her passport and threatened to force her into prostitution if she complained about him.

149. Diamond baron gifts 70 cars to staff: Employees rewarded for achieving annual targets; 30 others got cash

Surat: The diamond industry in Surat may not be passing through the most dazzling phases in its history, but a city-based diamond baron has gifted brand new Chevrolet-Beat as incentives to 70 of his employees for achieving their annual targets. Ironically, several of these artisans do not even know how to drive. "Thirty of the artisans were given cash, because some of them had to pay home loans, while others wanted to

Laughter as such doesn't say too much.
The burden of self is lightened when I laugh at myself – *Rabindranath Tagore.*

buy gold jewellery for their wives. We hope this would motivate other diamond polishers to do better," said Dholakia, who has a diamond-cutting and polishing unit at Varachha in Surat.

150. CM kin to chairman's child, Haryana Civil Services all in family

At-least two-third of the 30 candidates selected to Haryana Civil Service posts this year (2013) are relatives of political leaders, including Chief Minister Bhupinder Singh Hooda, and influential bureaucrats. The candidates selected by the Haryana Civil Service Commission (HCSC) include the daughter of the HPSC chairman, a daughter of Hooda's nephew and the son-in-law of the state power minister. HPSC Chairman Manbir Singh, however, defended the selections. "The selections were done solely on merit. All relationships of the selected candidates with the so-called high and mighty are only co-incident." Asked about selection of his own daughter; he said, "I recused myself from the interview of my daughter. Anybody can interview her and see her brilliance. Chief Minister said he played no role in the selection.

151. Docs use music to raise awareness on disease

New Delhi: It is not unusual to find doctors discussing medicine or diseases, but when they choose entertainment as a mode to raise awareness about a particular disease, it draws considerable attention. Doctors from different specialisations came together to raise awareness about rarely discussed celiac disease. Organised by The Celiac Society Centre, the event had doctors talking about the disease and the need for correct diagnosis. To make sure their message got across, they paired it up with a musical performance. Celiac disease is a condition in which the individual is intolerant to gluten (a protein found in

Laughter brings inner energy to the fore.
The first thing in the morning to do is to laugh, the very first thing.

cereals such as wheat). If undiagnosed, it can prove to be fatal or even lead to cancer. The treatment requires the patient to go on a gluten-free diet, a doctor at the event said.

152. Former army chief's adopted son to join unit

New Delhi: He was born in the shadow of massacre and spent his early years staring at an uncertain future. Life held there was an unexpected reversal of fortune when former army chief General J.J. Singh decided to adopt the seven-year-old-son of a poor carpenter in 1997 when he was then a brigadier.

Sixteen years later, the boy who used to sleep under the bed as he was afraid of terrorists, will don two stars on his epaulette as a lieutenant. And the honour of 'piping' (unravelling) the stars on Kuljit's shoulders will go to General J.J. Singh and his wife Anupama, who are travelling to the Indian Military Academy (IMA) in Dehradun for his passing out parade. As a tribute to the general, Kuljit has decided to join the 9 Maratha Light Infantry, a unit once commanded by the former chief.

General J.J. Singh, who has two children of his own, said, "It's a big day in our lives, Kuljit has overcome all obstacles to give his life a new direction." Kuljit's real mother, his fiancee and sister will also attend the parade. Singh adopted the another child in 2006 – James Kelengoto, an 11-year-old boy from the small town of Khuzama in insurgency-hit Nagaland. James had to go through a lot after his father died and mother remarried, leaving him and his four sisters to fend for themselves. James has also joined the army as soldier. He is determined to become an officer like his older 'brother' Kuljit. **Exemplary deed by former army chief.**

Laughter can be classified according to intensity, the chukle, the utter, the giggle, the chortle, the cackle, the belly laugh, the sputtering burst.

153. SC comes to rescue of HC judge's daughter Allows her to go with the person of her choice.

New Delhi: Asserting that marriage for an adult is an absolute matter of choice, the Supreme Court put an end to the ordeal of a sitting Rajasthan High Court Judge's daughter, who alleged she was forcibly confined inside the house for her wish to marry a man she chose. A Bench led by Justice H.L. Dattu asked the Rajasthan Police to ensure safety of the woman and reunite her with her boyfriend, who belonged to a different caste. "Keeping in view of the welfare of the girl and the fact that she has already attained majority, we say that she is at liberty to take her own future decisions regarding choice of marriage," said the court.

The woman told the court that she had no complaints or ill-will against her parents but she wanted to go with her boyfriend Siddharth Mukherjee since she wanted to marry him. The court recorded her statement and allowed her to go with the person of her choice.

154. Forty-three (43,000) applications for 300 Gujarat govt. assistant junior clerk jobs

Ahmedabad: Prashant Vala (not his real name), 27, who completed his Masters in Engineering (ME) in 2011 with distinction, works as an assistant professor at a self-financed engineering college in Gandhinagar for a monthly salary of ₹38,000. He is among the many MEs, MBAs, MCAs and other post-graduate who have applied for the post of assistant junior clerk at the Ahmedabad Municipal Corporation (AMC) – a job that requires only a second-class graduate and pays much less. While there are only 300 vacancies, the AMC has received

***Laughter can bring a new perspective** – Christopher Durang.*
Why is laughter so difficult to me?

43,000 applications, including from 14,000 post-graduates, many having completed professional courses like ME, Masters in Business Administration (MBA), Masters in Science (MSc), Masters in Computer Applications and Masters in Social Welfare (MSW).

155. UP govt. on a holiday spree, key word 'caste'

Lucknow: To keep the people happy, Romans gave them bread and circus. The Uttar Pradesh government gives holidays. Not just any holiday – but ones that confirm religion and caste, never mind the Supreme Court ban on caste politics. Since March 2012, the SP government has declared four brand new holidays – the latest being on December 23 in the honour of Chaudhary Charan Singh, supposedly to cool off the rising Jat tempers after the recent Muzaffarnagar riots. The other three were on April 5, Nishadraj Jayanti, May 17 for Ajmer Urs and October 29, Valmiki Jayanti. On the other, those on the bad books of the government had had their holidays pushed to the "restricted section", or worse, scrapped. Already, BSP founder Kanshiram and Dr. B.R. Ambedkar have had their names struck off the holiday list. "The government is indulging in holiday politics" said a grumpy BSP leader.

156. Resident doctor films woman colleague while bathing, held

Mumbai: A 27-year-old resident doctor studying at Bombay Hospital in South Mumbai was arrested for allegedly filming a woman doctor while she was bathing. The police said the cell phone used by the accused, Jayesh Shah, to commit the crime has also been seized. Shah had used the mobile to film other women doctors earlier, too, they added. The police said Shah positioned his cell phone over the partition that separates each cubicle. "She soon noticed a hand holding camera over the partition and raised an alarm. Shah was nabbed by other women doctors," said Narendra Singh, senior inspector, Azad Maidan police station.

157. Panchayat awards ₹10,000 for minor's rape, bars family from going to police!

Muzaffarpur: The compensation for minor girl's rape is just ₹10,000, or it will appear so if the decision of a panchayat committee of the district is to be believed. Rajwada panchayat of Mushahari block of the district decided to provide ₹10,000 to the family of a minor rape victim as compensation. It also barred the victim's family from registring FIR with the local police station. The shocking incident came to light when the victim's family somehow managed to reach Mushahari police station to lodge a complaint. The Mushahari police have raided the house of the rape accused after registering the case, but the culprits are absconding. "A panchayat was called when the matter was reported to it. They imposed a fine of ₹10,000 on the accused, while asking them to pay ₹3,000 at once. But I refused their proposal," mother of the victim said, adding that her refusal infuriated them.

158. Poor man prefers death to treasure stolen by son

Thiruvananthapuram: Thrippalur resident K. Radhakrishnan got a rude shock . He and his family members returned from the neighbourhood temple to find 272 gms. of gold jewellery missing. He got a bigger, albeit a more pleasant shock four days later – lying outside the main door of his house was a nicely wrapped package and in it was almost all of the missing gold with an apology note

***Laughter can help relieve tension in even the heaviest of matters** – Allen Klein.*
***That laughter costs too much which is purchased by the sacrifice of decency** – Quintilian.*

from the father of the thief. The missing gold is worth around ₹8 lakh. The writer of the note explained that the reason his son robbed Radhakrishnan was to fund his (father's) bypass surgery. But, he said, when he learnt what his son had done he was horrified and since he preferred death to stolen treasure he decided to return the gold to its rightful owner. Apologising for his son's action, the father also sought forgiveness and even assured that the missing 48 gms would be returned in the next couple of days. Meanwhile, Radhakrishnan has said if the case is genuine he will help fund the heart surgery.

159. HC orders woman to pray at Rajghat for a week for lying in court

New Delhi: The Delhi High Court has directed a woman, who was held guilty of making a false statement about her marital status under oath, to "repent her sin" by praying at Rajghat for at least four hours every day for a week at the memorial. "The conduct of the respondent is contumacious, as in the face of the court, she kept telling lies after lies. Also she had the audacity to take a false stand when her statement was recorded in court on oath," observed the court of Justice Kailash Gambhir and Justice Indermeet Kaur in its order. Though the apology was accepted by the court, she has also been guilty of contempt of court, and has also been directed to deposit ₹2,000 as fine to the Mahatma Gandhi Trust.

160. Separate tuition sessions for boys, girls in Srinagar State directive follows rape of minor by tutor in private centre

Srinagar: Following a state government directive, private tuition centres in Srinagar will hold separate sessions for

***Laughter does not seem to be a sin, but it leads to sin** – St. John Chrysostom.*
The sound of laughter is most sought after.

girls in the morning (after 8.30 am) and boys in the afternoon. The directive follows the rape of a minor student by a tutor. G.N. Var, chairman of Coaching Centres Association, said: "We have agreed to all the demands made by the government."

161. W. Champaran panchayat bans cellphones for girls

Patna: A village council in West Champaran has banned the use of mobile phones by unmarried girls, said a council member. The decision was taken at a meeting of Somgarh panchayat (council) in West Champaran district. The panchayat also threatened to impose heavy fine on the girls' families if they violated the diktat, said Zakir Ansari, husband of the village council head. "The decision was taken with approval of hundreds of villagers," said Ansari who works as the de facto head of the council. He said all families have been told to ensure that the decision is not violated. However, Bihar panchayati raj minister Bhim Singh said a panchayat has no right to impose ban on the use of mobile phones by girls or prevent them from keeping mobile phones.

162. School Chairman in custody for rape

Bhopal: The chairman of Maharishi Vidya Mandir Schools, Girish Chandra Verma, 53, was sent to police custody on a three-day remand on rape charges levelled against him by a former teacher of the school at Bhopal. Verma was arrested by police from his Bhopal bungalow; nine month after the woman lodged a complaint with Mahila police station accusing him of rape and sexual harassment.

One must laugh before one is happy or one may die without ever having laughed at all *– La Bruyere.*

---

163. Your house is a major source of pollution

Fatal: Pollution at home gives you respiratory, heart disease.

New Delhi: Contrary to public perception, air pollution is not just limited to outsiders. It remains even when you step inside. People living in poorly-ventilated homes face the added risk from indoor air pollutions – smoking, cooking flames, suspended particulate matter, mould, dust-mites and animal dander. Smoking at home is the biggest health hazard, especially in poorly-ventilated apartments. Passive intake of smoke is equally harmful and the bi-products linger on curtains and other articles in the house for very long. Those whose houses are located on the main road with heavy traffic movement can throw windows open very early in the morning for about an hour to let fresh air in.

164. Cop suspended for sloganeering during swearing-in-ceremony

New Delhi: A constable posted with the Delhi Armed Police Battalion was suspended for allegedly climbing the barricades at the Ramlila Maidan to shout slogans during Delhi CM Arvind Kejriwal oath-taking ceremony.

The constable was heard shouting that the Delhi Police should be brought under the Delhi government and that there was corruption. However, officers claimed that the reason for suspending him was his over-enthusiasm and him encouraging the public to follow suit. Joint Commissioner of Police (Central Range) Sandeep Goel said, "Despite repeated requests by the rest of the staff to get off the barricade, Rajesh Kumar continued shouting slogans. This act could have led members of the public

One should take good care not to grow too wise for so great a pleasure of life as laughter – *Joseph Addison.*

to follow suit. He was immediately removed and has been suspended."

165. Bihar: Villagers kill 12-year-old boy for stealing phone recharge-voucher, gutkha

Patna: A 12-year-old boy was beaten to death for stealing a mobile phone recharge voucher and gutkha worth ₹300 in a village in Purnia district. The police registered a case against eight people. The incident took place at Thadi village after two village boys allegedly stole the recharge voucher and gutkha from village shop. Pintu (13) and Chhotu (12) were produced before a village panchayat. After the two "confessed" to the crime, Pintu's father begged a panchayat member to forgive his son. While he was pardoned, there was no one to defend Chhotu as his mother was away. He was then reportedly beaten up in the presence of the panchayat. He succumbed to his injuries. Purnia SP Ajit Kumar Satyarthi confirmed the incident and called it a possible case of 'mob justice.'

166. In 97% rape cases, accused known to victim, police data reveals

New Delhi: In 97 per cent of the rape cases reported this year (2013), the crime was committed by a person known to the victim, police data reveals. In 40 per cent cases, the crime was committed by a family member or neighbour, data shows.

167. SC upholds sacking of CRPF personnel for 'cowardice'

New Delhi: The Supreme Court has upheld the dismissal of three CRPF men for display of "cowardice" and "dereliction of duty" during an ambush by militants in Assam 12 years ago in

***Laughter gives us distance. It allows us to step back from an event, deal with it and then move on** – Bob Newhart.*

which five personnel of the paramilitary force were killed. It was found that instead of repulsing attack, the two head constables fled the scene.

168. No govt. unfettered discretion says Supreme Court

New Delhi: The Supreme Court held that no government or authority, including the "chief justice" has unfettered discretion" or "unaccountable action" and any such exercise is subject to judicial review. A bench of Justice R.V. Raveendran and Justice Markandeya Katju held that in a democracy where the rule of law prevailed, even the prerogative power is subject to judicial review.

169. A bridge for all but public representatives

Darbhanga: The residents of Kamalpur-Brahmotar Ghat, a village under Pirri Panchayat of Bahadurpur block in Darbhanga, finally built a bamboo bridge (locally known as 'chachri' bridge) over Kamla river. The bridge was thrown open strictly for 'public' The villagers, however, proclaimed in a banner ***(Setu Par Janpratinidhi Sansad, Vidhayakon Ka*** **PRAVESH VARJIT*)*** that local MP and MLAs should keep out from crossing over the bridge! Two months have passed since then. It is not known whether people's representative ever tied to defy their diktat! They also announced to boycott forthcoming parliamentary elections to press their demand seeking construction of an RCC bridge on the spot.

Laughter has no greater enemy than emotion. Laughter requires 'a momentary anaesthesia of the heart – *Henri Bergson.*

---

170. Nepal man held for tattooing pic. of friend's wife on chest

Kathmandu: A 35-year-old Nepalese man has been arrested for tattooing the likeness of his friend's wife on his chest, **the first case of its kind in the country.**

Kumar Kesi from Kavre district east of Kathmandu claimed that his love had grown after he tattooed the woman's picture on his chest. "Kumar has been kept in police custody under the Public Offence Act as there is no law related to the act of tattooing a woman's picture," Police Officer Arun Kumar Bisi said. Kumar said he fell in love with the woman after she was introduced to him by her husband four years ago. "We began in love each other after our meetings," he claimed. Kumar had used a photo given to him by the woman some years ago for the tattoo, which features the woman with her hair tied and a big 'tika' on her forehead. After he showed off the tattoo to his friends during Diwali last year (2013), word about it spread like wildfire. He said, "she used to meet me in Banepa and Kathmandu on the pretext that she was ill, and had to go for check up."The husband forced his wife to disclose their relationship and filed a case against Kumar, Following the complaint, police arrested Kumar recently.

171. Assam changes local time by one hour, sets clock back by 150 years

Guwahati/New Delhi: After 66 years of following the Indian Standard Time (IST), Assam has decided to follow the **"chaibagan time"** - a daylight schedule British tea planters introduced over 150 years ago – despite the lack of a Central nod. The north-eastern states see sunrise – and sunset – well over an hour before Mumbai. The IST forces them to lose

Laughter helps us bond with others.
The loud laugh, that speaks the vacant mind - *Goldsmith.*

daylight hours and work late into the evening. Advocates of dual time zone say it would help increase productivity, reduce power usage and curb alcoholism. "These states have been asking New Delhi for a separate time zone. We have now decided to set our clocks to bagaan time." Assam Chief Minister on Wednesday. Set one hour ahead of IST, bagaan time is still followed by tea estates, colleries and the oil industry. Even the 112 -year-old Digboi Refinery follows it.

172. Here, villagers hurl abuses to ward off evil spirits

Kullu (HP): It's a festival of hurling choicest abuses at each other. Old-timers say it's a centuries old tradition that helps evil spirits at bay.

The Diyali festival was celebrated in Naggar village, known for Russian painter and philosopher Nicholas Roerich's estate and 25 km. from this town, where the locals participated. According to tradition, the festival, which marks invoking gods amid the beating of drums and blowing of trumpets, is celebrated on the night of new moon 'amavasya' (moonless night of the dark fortnight of a lunar month) (December 16 to January 13). As per the tradition, the first torch is lit at the Jagti Pat temple, located in Naggar village, the erstwhile capital of the Kullu rulers. From there, the locals take the flame lit on twigs to their village home for lighting. "The locals take out processions through the villages, carrying a man on a pole with sheep horns adorning his head. During the processions, they sing abusive phrases. The abuses help warding off evil spirits," said octogenarian Dule Ram. The womenfolk are barred to participate in the procession. After the culmination of the procession at the Jagti Pat temple, the temple priest read out the forecast of the year ahead.

Laughter helps you to relax more.
Laughter followed the gloom and love began to bloom.

---

173. CBSE cracks down on SMS lingo in examinations

Patna: 'Writing lyk dis mite gt u aprctn 4m frnz.'

But, if it is high marks you crave at the CBSE (Central Board of Secondary Education) board examinations scheduled to start on March 1, try not to sound cool in pulverising decent words. In short, do not use the SMS lingo! The CBSE has informed all students set to appear in the class 10 and 12 examinations in advance, to refrain from using shortened words in their answer sheets or else they are bound to lose marks. The notification comes in the wake of complaints forwarded by teachers of various CBSE schools, saying that 90% of students used the SMS language in writing their answers in the summative and formative assessments conducted by schools. "It has become a habit of student to use abbreviated words in their examinations. While it is excused when they take notes in class, writing like this in the examinations is not permitted," the teachers say. **Hop u gt it. Al d best!**

174. Man sues son for inter-caste marriage

Patna: A man in Bihar has disowned his son and filed defamation case against him for marrying out of caste.

Sidhnath Sharma, a Patna lawyer, also asserted that his son Sushant Jasu could no longer use his name and will have to pay ₹10,000 copyright fees every time he used it. Filing defamation suit of ₹1 crore against his son in the court at Danapur, Patna, Sharma said, "My image and honour was hurt by my son, who solemnised inter-caste marriage against wishes, now he must compensate for it." Jasu, who works for the central government as a senior tax assistant in Gujrat's Palmpur town, married a Danapur girl who works in a private bank on November 19, 2013.

Laughter improves your blood flow and increases your immune system by 28 per cent.

An angry Sharma said, "I and my wife spent time and money to nurse my son for years but he betrayed us. He fell in love with a girl who came into his life two years ago only." He claimed his son act has **ended nearly 400-year-old family tradition of marrying within their own caste.** In Bihar, inter caste marriages, though encouraged by the government, are still largely considered taboo and those who do it generally face hostility from families and society. In a bid to encourage such marriages, the state government last year decided to double the incentive for it. Under the scheme, a woman marrying out of caste will now get ₹50,000 instead of ₹25,000.

175. First Ramayana Varsity in Vaishali

Patna: After the world's largest Ram Temple, the Virat Ramayan Mandir in East Champaran district of north Bihar, the Patna-based Mahavir Mandir Trust now plans one of its kind "Ramayan University" at Biddupur in Vaishali district. "It will be a modern university with Wi-Fi campus and online facility," said Acharya Kishore Kunal, chairman of the temple trust.

The university would impart specialised education in astrology, astrophysics, Hindu mythology like Vedas and Upnishads, Karmkand, Sanskrit, and much more and strive to preserve and promote the literature of the Ramayan in the whole world; whether it is in Sanskrit, Hindi, vernacular texts or the languages of South Eastern Asian countries. "Apart from reviving all that India once epitomised, the courses will also provide greater employ-ability. At present, there is a dearth of knowledgeable priests for rituals. The university will prepare scholarly priests. There will be high-level research on Ayurveda.

176. Clerics not to conduct nikah of dowry seekers

Patna: Alarmed over the trend of dowry among Muslims,"We have decided not to conduct nikah (marriage) for those who take and give dowry in the district," said Qazi Maulana Mansur Alam, who heads Muslim organisation Imarat-e-Sharia of Biharsharif in Nalanda. "It is a historic move to discourage dowry and create awareness. It is a kind of social boycott to warn dowry takers," he said. Alam said after this decision was successfully implemented in Nalanda, about 100 km. from Patna, they would request Imams of other districts across Bihar to start similar campaigns. The Muslim community has welcomed this move against dowry. "It is a positive step to counter increasing dowry and create awareness".

177. Pre-marital sex immoral, no religion permits it, says fast-track court judge

New Delhi: A Delhi court has said pre-marital sex is 'immoral' and against the "tenets of every religion", while holding that every act of sexual intercourse between two adults on the promise of marriage does not become rape.

Additional Session Judge Virendra Bhat, who delivered the order on December 20, 2013, also held that a woman, especially grown up, educated and office-going, who has sexual intercourse on the assurance of marriage does so "at her own peril," "She must be taken to understand the consequences of her act and must know that there is no guarantee that the boy would fulfil his promise." "He may or may not do so. She must understand that she is engaging in an act which not only is immoral but also against tenets of every religion. No religion in the world allows pre-marital sex," the court said, while acquitting an employee with a multinational company of the charges of rape.

Laughter is a flowering. If Buddha was the seed, then Hotei is the flower on the same tree. People used to call him the Laughing Buddha.

The 29-year old man, a resident of Punjab, was arrested after a month when the women lodged a complaint of rape against him in May 2011. In her complaint, the woman, who is an orphan, had alleged that the man, whom she had met through a chat website in July 2006, used to have physical relations with her on several occasions by promising to marry her. When the woman got pregnant in 2008, the man instead of marrying her, asked her to abort the foetus by saying that he would marry her once his sisters get married, she had alleged. She also told the police that even after the sisters of the accused got married, he did not marry her and instead he and his parents abused and harassed her.

The court looked into the fact that the woman held a job of a 'secretarial and administrative nature with a reputed company' while observing that she could not have been misled by the man's promises. "She was an independent lady and had been residing on rent alone in Bangalore since the year 2003. Hence, I consider that she was intelligent enough to understand moral quality and consequences of her act and there were no chances of their being misled by any assurance given to her by the accused," the judge said.

178. Medical community paid ₹40 lakh for negligence last year

New Delhi: Accused of apathy and corporate greed, the medical community was, over the last year, made to pay a total of ₹40 lakh in compensation for negligence.

"These days corporate culture has taken over the basic fundamentals of the (medical) service. They are indulging in unscrupulous procedures for the purpose of making money at

Parents, teachers, bosses commanders all in the society wants you to be serious. Laughter is dangerous and rebellious, insult. Seriousness is considered to be honour, respect.

the cost of the patient," N.A. Zaidi, president of the East-District Consumer Forum, observed while considering a hospital to pay ₹5 lakh in compensation for an unnecessary and unsuccessful cyst-removal surgery which worsened the health of an 18-year old.

179. 'No need to call us my lord or lordship, sir is good enough'

New Delhi: "All that judges need is a respectful and dignified way of addressing them. You don't need to call us "my lord" or "lordship" always; calling us 'sir' is good enough for us." This was the message the Supreme Court sent out to lawyers and litigants.

A Bench of justices H.L. Dattu and S.A. Bobde said it was the choice of the lawyers how to address them but the court was clear that it only wanted a respectable address to the chair. "To address the court, what do we want? Only a respectable way of addressing. You call (judges) it your honour, it is accepted. You call lordship, it is accepted. These are some of the appropriate way of expression and we accept everything," the Bench said.

180. HC steps in to protect Bhabua minors

Bhabua : Patna high court Justice Navin Sinha directed the Kaimur district legal services authority (DLSA) to provide legal and other help required by three minors tortured by their own father and effect action against him on the basis of their complaints 'within 24 hours.'

The three children – the eldest an intermediate student, her 14-year old brother and eight-year-old sister had been subjected to cruelty and even attempt to rape by their father after their mother died last September, 2013 and a step mother was brought

Laughter is a mechanism everyone has; laughter is part of universal human vocabulary. **Laugh like a hyena** – *William Shakespeare.*

in. The latest trouble that they are facing is courtesy the private school where her two siblings are currently studying. The school authorities warned them that would be ousted as they had not deposited the school fee for the last several months.

Secretary DLSA-cum-sub-judge1 Ramesh Chandra Dwivedi sent a letter to family judge Manmohan Choudhary with a request for interim maintenance to the victim girl and her siblings for their quick rehabilitation.

181. Rat bites woman passenger in Rajdhani

Gaya: The railways appear to be losing the fight against pests and rodents on trains. A 55-year-old woman was bitten by a rat in H-1 compartment of New Delhi-Kolkata Rajdhani at Sasaram station. As the train was moving, irate passengers pulled the chain and stopped it.

Roma Chaterjee, who was asleep, suffered a cut to a toe and screamed out. Passengers, who rushed to her help, kicked up a ruckus when the travelling ticket examiner said she could get treated when the train reached Gaya. As the train had already started to move, passengers pulled the chain. "The incident happened after the train reached Gaya junction. We brought a doctor who was on duty at the station. She gave an injection to prevent infection and administered first aid," said a Railway Protection Force (RPF) official. The train was further delayed when passengers demanded that the doctor issue a medical certificate saying the woman was bitten by a rat.

182. Disciplined clapping

Patna: Usually grave of disposition, Chief Minister Nitish Kumar is given to displays of a great sense of humour from time to time. He did so at Patna Women's College annual day function.

When the chief minister's turn to speak came, he praised the institution's growth. "And for discipline," he went on with a smile, "Well, what can one say? Here, the girls clap only when the principal prompts them to do so!" At the audience broke into laughter, the principal, Sister Doris D'Souza, blushed. A keen observer, Kumar had noticed how the principal exhorted the students to clap at every strategic juncture, during the function. The students, he found, were prompt in their response to the signal from the principal.

183. Cops send unconscious man for post-mortem

Dhanbad: In a bizarre case of negligence, Dhanbad police failed in identifying a dead person from a living one, and sent a 60-year-old unknown male for post-mortem without obtaining his death certificate from the concerned doctors. The 'unknown' beggar was found unconscious near Dhanbad main post office which is located next to the Dhanbad police station. The police, instead taking him to hospital, set him directly to a post mortem house. Incidentally, the staff at the post-mortem house noticed that the person was alive and inform the officer-in-charge of the police station. The police then, grasping the sensitivity of the matter, called an ambulance. Unfortunately, the person in the crux of the fiasco, died due to unknown medical problem.

184. 'Retired' goddesses of Kathmandu to get pension

Kathmandu: Retirement has its perks. Former Kumaris of Kathmandu, pre-pubescent girls worshipped as living goddesses and removed from their position once they reach puberty, would agree.

Laughter is a tranquilizer with no side effects *– Arnold H. Glasow.*
There is little success where there is little laughter *– Andrew Carnegie.*

The metropolitan council of Nepal's capital, Kathmandu Metropolitan City Office, has decided to provide retirement benefits to those former living goddesses as part of its fresh budget allocation. Beginning mid-July, the start of Nepal's fiscal year, eight former kumaris would receive monthly sum of ₹10,000 (₹6,250) as pension. This is a gesture to extend our tribute to the former Kumaris. This is also an initiative to preserve our cultural heritage.

185. 'Only 47% in Class V can read Class II text'

New Delhi: Over 96 per cent of children in rural India may now be enrolled in schools, but what they learn is a big question. With the exception of a few, learning outcome in most states remains dismal, with students unable to read a Class II-level text or solve basic arithmetic problems. There are some of the findings of the ninth annual Status of Education Report, 2013, the largest household survey of children in rural India conducted by NGO Pratham.

186. Court dismisses impersonation charge against man

New Delhi: LAST YEAR (2013), the CBI booked Sanjeev Kumar on the charge of impersonation. Kumar had allegedly claimed he was an Officer on Special Duty (OSD) with the Central Vigilance Commission (CVC).

He moved a session court against the charge, claiming since there was no one named Sanjeev Kumar posted as an OSD in the CVC, he had not imposed anyone. The court quashed the charge of impersonation against him.

Laughter is an instant vacation *- Milton Berle.* ***They laugh that win.***
You enjoy it more if you can laugh at it *- Unknown Source.*

The CBI argued that in addition to availing gift facility from a store, it had recovered two letters from his car, addressed to Kumar as OSD, CVC. The judge dismissed the argument, observing that "the case against the accused can be described at stage of 'preparation', not even reaching at the stage of attempt."

187. Dog shakes off dogged pursuit, takes off with ₹4 lakh cash

Patna: Every dog they say, has its day. And what a day, a street dog enjoyed when it entered a house in Line Bazaar locality of Mirganj in Gopalganj district and actually ran away with ₹4 lakh kept in a polythene wrap. The whole town is now running and gunning for the dog which is traceless.

Nakched Mian, a green grower, does not know how to react to the situation, where he can neither press charges, nor actually explain away the presence of such huge cash in his house. He has, however, gathered his wits to file a station diary since the police told him 'a criminal charge is out of question.' Desperate, Nakched has started a hunt for the 'mercenary' dog, but to no avail. His plight has turned worse since his complaint has just drawn ridicule and laughs. But then, the grapevine has it that all dogs were under scrutiny by bounty hunters who hope to catch the dog and keep the cash. In his written complaint, Nakched has mentioned that his son, living in a foreign country, had sent him ₹3 lakh while another ₹1 lakh came from his business.

"I had kept ₹4 lakh in a polythene bag. It was on my bed. As I went to wash my hands at the hand pump, I saw a dog running away with the bag. I gave it a hot chase, but it disappeared in the locality", he added. Nakched said he had kept the money for

---

Few persons realise that health actually varies according to the amount of laughter.

---

payment to someone. "I had bought a piece of land, but now I cannot pay the money", he added.

Police, however, tried to console him, saying that the dog might have run away with polythene mistaking it for some food item. Later, ₹1.40 lakh was found recovered near Nakched's house following a police search in the area.

188. Incident which got Jaipur girl selected for bravery award fake: Police

Jaipur: A 16-year-old- girl, who was selected for the National Bravery award for bravery for foiling a bid by two men to abduct her, is in the centre of a controversy. Police have denied that any such incident took place and have filed a closure report to this effect in a court after a probe.

The Class XI student had hogged headlines in local newspapers by claiming that she fought off two men, who tried to push her into an SUV and kidnap her. Her parents claimed that she showed extraordinary courage in saving herself from them on Janpath road in Shyam Nagar for which she was selected for the prestigious Geeta Chopra Award.

189. Govt. servant's wife has right to know husband's salary: CIC

New Delhi: Wives of government servants have a 'right' to know salary particulars of their husband, especially for the purpose of maintenance and these details should also be made public by their offices as mandated under suo-moto disclosure clause of the RTI Act, the Central Information Commission has held. The Commissioner further said that the details about a government employee's salary is

---

I love people who make me laugh. Life is better when you are laughing. We are paying very high price for taking life seriously. Now it's time to take laughter seriously.

---

no third party information and these have to be voluntarily disclosed under Section 4(1)(b)(x) of the RTI Act.

190. PMC commissioner seeks info. Through RTI to fight 'injustice'

Patna: In an unusual development, an IAS officer has taken recourse to the Right to Information (RTI) Act to elicit some information from his controlling department headed by another IAS officer. In news for his drive against irregular high rises in the city, Patna Municipal Corporation (PMC) Commissioner Kuldip Narayan, a 2005 batch IAS officer, has filed a petition under the RTI Act to fight what he called "injustice meted out to him by the controlling department." Apparently let down by the continued apathy of the urban development department towards his repeated reminders, Narayan has taken recourse to the RTI to know the source of the letter issued by an undersecretary by which he was asked to pay a legal retainer of the PMC from his salary.

It may be mentioned here that officials of the department as well as the PMC mayor have been insisting on removing H.S. Himkar, a lawyer on the panel of the civic body. The commissioner, however, refused to oblige them citing the powers vested with him under various provisions of the related acts, including the Bihar Municipal Act, 2008. In his previous letters to the government, Narayan noted Himkar had been actively protecting the interest of the PMC in the court of law, especially after the corporation tried to stop rampant violation of the stipulated building codes following orders of the Patna high court. The stringent orders are said to have badly hit the real estate business worth thousands of crores of rupees in the state capital.

If you laugh a lot, when you get older your wrinkles will be in the right place. Laugh as much as you breathe and love as long as you live.

---

191. The only Indian winner in NZ is in the stands, ₹52 lakh richer

Hamilton: New Zealand: There was particularly loud cheer in the stands at the Seldon Park when New Zealand pinch-hitter Corey Anderson walked out to bat in ODI against India. After two-hour break with fewer than seven overs to go, the spectators were hoping to get their money's worth - and may be, some money as well.

A lot of money actually - 100,000 NZ dollars (about ₹52 lakh) to be precise - through a promotional scheme which required them to catch with one hand any hit sailing past the fence. And by the time he walked back to the pavilion, the potential IPL millionaire, Anderson had left a 22-year old Indian origin New Zealander richer beyond his dreams. His fourth six, which came off Ishant Sharma, nestled in Jatinder Singh's right hand on the embankment beyond long-on fence.

As the stadium roared, TV cameras zoomed in on an ecstatic Jatinder who was now surrounded by fellow spectators. The youngster's life, as he knew it, had changed.

"To be honest, I got up and didn't think it was going to make it as far as me. I thought it was going to land short, so then I sort of gave up on it, and then it kept going and next thing know it was in my right hand. Really, happened so fast. I started jumping up and down, that's not me. Normally I am quite reserved," said Jatinder, a fourth-generation Indian whose roots are in Punjab. His father own a farm in T Aroha near Hamilton, while his mother, who is from Amritsar, is a housewife. The scheme that made it happen, 'Catch-a-Million', was launched by beer brand Tui for the 10 **ODI** starting with the New Zealand-West Indies Match on December 26, 2013.One of the requirements is that participants have

Laughter is the best medicine but if you laugh for no reason, you need medicine. Everybody laughs in the same language.

to come to a match wearing the official orange-coloured Tui T-shirt. Only 250 shirts are sold from the merchandise store at the venue of each match. Jatinder is the second person to take the 100,000 dollar catch after Michael Mortan caught the New Zealand-West Indies game, also in Hamilton, on January 8, 2014.

"I should have thanked Corey actually; I do owe him a lot. And I owe a lot to the bowler as well. So thank you, Ishant Sharma."

192. School awards extra points to vegetarians, non-smokers

New Delhi: Minority schools in the capital may have got the go-ahead from the High Court to set own parameters. But one school has taken nursery admission to a whole new level by showing preference for children whose parents are vegetarians, non-smokers and teetotallers.

The decision of the school, Mahavir Model School, to allot five points for each category - vegetarians, non-smokers and teetotallers- has met with surprise from admission seekers.

The move has also prompted questions on the purpose of setting such a criteria. "We are a Jain minority school. Jains are very strict about their diet. Vegetarianism is a way of life for our community. Smoking and consuming alcohol is not good for anyone. Gandhiji said to himself. So, we have decided to give points to anyone who doesn't practise any of the three," Principal S.L. Jain said.

193. Aadhaar is not a proof of citizenship: Nilekani

Bangalore: Aadhaar is not a proof of citizenship, but a basic identity for a person to avail himself or herself of various

Laughter is by definition healthy *– Doris Lessing.*
True wit never made a man laugh *– Chesterfield.*

benefits provided by the government said Chairman of Unique Identification Authority of India (UIDAI) Nandan Nilekani. Speaking to presspersons after visiting the Traffic Management Centre, Mr. Nilekani described Aadhaar as the one of the world's biggest social inclusion projects that aims to help beneficiaries get over ₹3,000 crore subsidies provided by the government.

194. When Patna rickshaw puller outshone 'VIPs'

New Delhi: A New Delhi Municipal Council maternity hospital was inaugurated at Lodhi Colony. There was difference in his sombre government function though. Instead of the chief minister or any other dignitary, Vijay Baba, a homeless rickshaw puller, who hails from Patna inaugurated it. As he sat flanked by AAP supporters waiting for the function to start, Baba looked content and excited to get the opportunity to be the **"chief guest"**. "It is a good day, may be one of the best days of my life. How can often does a common man like me get such an opportunity? Never in my dreams had I thought that I would be inaugurating with the chief minister by my side. It is a big honour," the 60-year-old said. He came in his own rickshaw from Connaught Place, where he lives with his 14-year-old son Suraj Kumar – one of the youngest campaigners of AAP in the Assembly polls – in a small plastic 'room' on the side of the road near Aulia Mosque. "Many people wanted me here in their cars. I said no, I will come in my own rickshaw, I am still an aam admi, " Baba, a native of Patna said, with a smile.

195. Social connect

Japanese First Lady Akie Abe surprised everyone with an unusual request on Saturday evening (25.01.2014). As she met Prime Minister Manmohan Singh's wife Gursharan Kaur

A child's giggle is worth one hundred pounds of gold *- Amy Leigh Mercree.*

in Hyderabad House for a separate one-on-one meeting, she is learnt to have asked her if she could post their picture on social media. Kaur smiled and gave her nod to the Japanese First Lady. Abe, who is very social media- savvy, posted their pictures within minutes on her Facebook page.

196. Wedding ceremony held at UP hospital

Vadodara: A wedding ceremony was solemnized on the premises of a hospital in Bharuch, UP on 24.01.2014 as the groom's father is bed-ridden following kidney failure. Irfan Rikshawala, got married to Samaiya Bombeywalla at the hospital in Bharuch. Irfan's marriage was to be solemnised on February 22 but was brought forward in view of his father's ill health.

197. Govt. to treat SMS as official record

New Delhi: People may soon be able to use SMS communication with government departments as a documentary proof while utilizing citizen services for making payments, registrations and various other schemes. Launching the "mobile seva" service, department of electronics and IT secretary J. Satyanarayana said, "Like railways, we have to bring in a system wherein by showing (transaction) SMS or, whatever be the case (like email), the proof on mobile is accepted as valid document. India has actually 90 crore mobile phone users."

198. Single women enjoy playing the 'PANK' Professional Aunt With No Kids' In Demand:

New Delhi: Web content writer Ayaani Dutta and her two teenage niece as from a mutual admiration society. She is their friend, confidante and their "chalta phirta (mobile) bank". In return, they shower unconditional love on their sprightly aunt. "With me, they get to do fun, freaky stuff – dance in the rain, streak their hair pink during vacation – things their mom would never allowed," says Dutta. She is among a growing breed of career women who opt out of marriage and motherhood but love to play mom, by proxy, to the children of siblings and friends, PANKs (professional aunt with no kids), in fact, enjoy the best of both worlds – the joy of mothering but few of its pangs.

Dutta is thrilled to be a PANK. "I would prefer maasi-dom any day to motherhood," says the 42-year-old who decided to stay single after a serious relationship went sour. PANKs enjoy a unique relationship with their 'children,' one that a parent could envy.

199. Fake surgery: 'Erring' doc held

Purnia: The doctor who conducted a fake surgery upon a patient and took money from him has been arrested. Confirming the arrest, the police said he was nabbed from Premnagar, Rupauli. Dr. P.K. Choudhary posted at Rupauli PHC was charged by Satyanarayan Sahni that the doctor had cheated him in the name of operation of hernia and administered sleep-inducing drugs to his son instead, and kept him at his clinic for three days. Later when it was discovered the doctor disappeared from the scene. Deepak Sahni was brought at the Rupauli PHC when the doctor after examining him suggested his father to admit the boy at his private clinic. Later, the doctor took fee and told Satyanarayan Sahni that Deepak had already been operated. When the father opened the bandage and found no cut mark, he complained about it to the doctor who allegedly told him it was a ***"Chhoo-mantar"*** operation.

200. Sleep a fundamental right, says court

New Delhi: The Delhi high court termed sound sleep as a fundamental right of citizens. The observation came while hearing a two-year-old petition by the residents of Vasant Kunj and surrounding areas, seeking a solution to noise pollution caused by landing of planes at the IGI airport's third runway.

Chief Justice Dipak Misra and Justice Sanjiv Khanna heard an audio-visual plea by the residents of Vasant Kunj, Masudpur and Rangpuri. The court also heard the Delhi International Airport Limited (DIAL) and Airport Authority of India (AAI).

While seeking an audio-visual presentation, the Bench said, "every citizen has a right to sleep peacefully in night and no noise shall disturb his/her sound sleep. The concept of sound sleep is associated with sound health, which is an inseparable facet of Article 21 of the Constitution."

201. Lack of toilet in govt. schools prompt 60% girls to drop out

Ranchi: In Jharkhand, the dropout rate of girls studying in government schools is around 10 per cent. This is because of the lack of toilets and urinals for girls. The UNICEF in 2010 had revealed that 33 lakh girls are out of school and one of the major reasons for this was that there were no separate toilets for them. A state report on education says that 65 per cent girls drop out after attending primary school.

The Right of Child to Free and Compulsory Education (RTE) Act, 2009, specifically mentions that schools should have separate toilets for girls and boys.

A maid that laughs is half taken.

202. Cycle culture

New Delhi: Justice Dalveer Bhandari is to leave for the Hague next month (June 2012) to join the International Court of Justice. Bhandari was perplexed when he received a phone call from Hague asking whether he would like a bicycle to be booked for him. In India, Justices are used to limousines and pilot cars and the thought that in the Hague, most people travel by cycles for short distances came as culture shock to the honourable judge.

203. House business

New Delhi: When Parliament is not able to transact any business due to disruption even during the extended winter session, the obvious question most people ask is, what purpose does it serve? "Well , it boost the revenues of both Assam and Bengal," contends Congress MP Mani Shankar Aiyar. How? The irrepressible Aiyar has a ready explanation to this too 'just look at the tea and coffee being consumed (by members without work)."

204. Shivering as exercise

Shivering in cold sparks a series of biochemical reactions that alter fat cells and bolsters metabolism, much as formal exercise does, according to a fascinating series of new experiments. The findings intimate that exercise and shivering are related in ways not previously suspected.

205. Three judicial officers face sack

RARE MOVE Patna High Court standing committee finds their act 'undesirable'.

Patna: In a rare move, the full court meeting of the Patna high court, presided over by the Chief Justice Rekha M. Doshit, approved the resolution based on a standing committee recommendation, to dismiss from service three senior judicial officers for their involvement in "undesirable activity."

The action follows a detailed inquiry after a news appeared in a Nepalese daily 'Udgosh' on January 29, 2013 regarding a raid in Metro Hotel, Biratnagar (Nepal) on January 2, 2013 in which the three judicial officers from Bihar were caught with some women and later released without recording their detention. The three judicial officers had allegedly crossed over to Biratnagar in Nepal after the 2013 Republic Day function. The three are Komal Ram, the then judicial magistrate, Araria (presently sub-judge, Nawada), Jitendra Nath Singh, the then additional district and session judge, Ara (presently ad hoc district and session judge, Ara) and Hari Niwas Gupta, the then principal judge, family court, Samastipur (presently principal judge, family court, Muzaffarpur). The state cabinet gave its nod to dismissal of three senior judicial officers from service on the recommendation of the Patna high court.

206. Doctor who developed chicken pox vaccine dies at 85

New York: Dr. Michiaki Takahashi, whose experience caring for his 3-year-old son after the boy contracted chicken pox led him to develop vaccine for the virus that is now used all over the world, died on December 23, 2013 in Osaka, Japan. He was 85.

Today, chicken pox – like other childhood diseases for which vaccines had been

A silence without laughter is dead, and laughter without silence is superficial. When both are together..... it is something phenomenal.

developed earlier, including measles, mumps, rubella and polio – is largely a thing of the past.

207. Creator of the world's most famous assault rifle AK-47 dies

New York: Lt. Gen. Mikhail T. Kalashnikov, the arms designer credited by the Soviet Union with creating the AK-47, the first in a series of rifles and machine guns that would indelibly associate his name with modern war and become the most abundant firearms ever made, died on 23rd December, 2013 in Izhevk, the capital of the Udmurtia republic, where he lived. He was 94. The weapon was designed to protect the motherland, not to be used by terrorists or thugs. "This is a weapon of defence and not a weapon for offence."

208. India's Greta Garbo, true star who knew how to play that role

New Delhi: For Hindi cinema fans, Suchitra Sen's name is synonymous with *Aandhi*, in which she played a character widely seen as presenting Indira Gandhi. She died at the age of 82.

209. Man stoned to death for protesting loud music

Purnia: A dispute over loud music being played on the public address system during late hours on the occasion of Saraswati Puja claimed one life in the district.

Vijay Sah alias Munna, 35, was stoned to death following an altercation that ensued after he requested the puja revellers to

Everything is funny as long as it happens to somebody else.

reduce the volume of the loudspeaker. The prime accused, Sonu, 19, in the case had earlier attacked his cousin Raja with stones, damaging one of his eyes, after differences over Saraswati Puja celebrations.

210. Three Patna students leave home "to catch Dawood"

Patna: Three students of reputed Patna School, influenced by a movie left home apparently to catch underworld don Dawood Ibrahim. They got the idea after watching Bollywood film D-Day, police said. "The three told police they wanted to earn a fast buck by catching Dawood and handing him over to the Government of India."

211. Seventy-five (75%) of parties fund from unknown sources

New Delhi: Over 75% of the funding received to political parties is from unknown donors. According to data analyzed by the Association for Democratic Reforms (ADR), the toal funds received by six national political parties between 2004-2005 and 2011-2012 was ₹4,895.96 crore of which only 8.9% was from known donors. Around ₹3,674.50 crore or 75.5% were anonymous contribution.

212. After 8 years in Jail, killer to be freed as juvenile

Mumbai: Eight years after a Mumbai boy was arrested for stabbing a man to death, the Bombay high court ordered the accused Raju Singh (name changed) to be released from prison deeming him to be a juvenile – below the age of 18 – at the time of the crime.

213. Hundred seventeen (117) women 'crorepatis' in Gujarat village give wings to dreams

Sanand: This tiny hamlet near motown Sanand may well have the largest conglomeration of women crorepatis in Gujarat. Of the 400-odd people who have become crorepatis overnight after the Gujarat Industrial Development Corporation paid hefty compensation for land, a little less than 30% - 117 – are women. One such woman is Kalayni Yadav (32), who has got a cheque of ₹85 crore in her name. Her mother Leela (56) got a cheque of ₹2.43 crore while father Ramsingh got ₹3.5 crore. Kalyani says her father has given the freedom to use a large percentage of the money to give wings to her dream of becoming an agro-entrepreneur, "I have a dream of running an agriculture processing unit.

214. Doctor granted divorce after wife locks fridge

Mumbai: A family court has granted divorce to a doctor couple married for 19-years on grounds of cruelty after he told to the court that she had repeatedly insulted him and had denied him food by locking up the refrigerator and deprived him of any eatables and water and every time he was forced to ask her for the key. The doctor claimed that he could only drive the car if she accompanied him or was using the car. The court accepted the doctor's contentions and passed an order ex-parte as the estranged wife did not appear in court. The former couple were married in January 1994 and had no children.

215. Poverty a mitigating ground to convert death to life term: SC

New Delhi: More than three decades after carving out 'rarest of rare' category of cases warranting award of death penalty, the Supreme Court found a new mitigating factor – poverty – to commute a convict's death penalty to life imprisonment.

A tailor was finding it difficult to make ends meet with his meager income and had a wife and three children, two sons and a daughter to support. One of the sons was suffering from asthma and needed constant medication. One night, he took a pair of scissors and repeatedly stabbed them. So vicious was the attack that the wife and two sons died without utter scream.

The injured girl asked the father why he was hurting all of them when they had not done anything. The man's fatherly instincts surfaced for a moment when he gave her water. But immediately afterwards, he tried to smother her with a pillow. Taking her to be dead, he bolted the door of the house from outside and went straight to the police station to confess.

216. Couple donating blood since 1993

Darbhanga: A couple - Dr. Bidhan Chandra Singh (56) and wife Sheela Singh - living in Bengali Tola under Laheriasarai police station in Darbhanga district has a unique way of paying tribute to Mahatma Gandhi. Every year the couple goes to the regional blood bank at DMCH and donates blood on October 2, and this has been going on since 1993.

217. Kids born out of wedlock have right to family pension

New Delhi: Children of divorced or those born to the illegally wedded wife of a deceased All-India Services Officer are entitled to get family pensions, according to new rules notified by the Centre.

I force myself to laugh at everything for fear of being obliged to weep.

---

218. Posing as lawyer not an offence, says court

New Delhi: Ravinder Pratap Singh allegedly dressed up in 'black suit, white shirt and a black tie' and habitually appears in courts, posing as an advocate. Irked by this impersonation, a retired Army major approached police and then the court, seeking an FIR against Singh. Both the forums turned him down on the grounds that wearing a lawyer's garb in court was not an offence under the criminal code.

219. 'Bride pregnant by another, marriage voidable'

Mumbai: A city court recently declared the marriage of a 30-year-old Indian Air Force employee voidable after he claimed he was forcibly married off in 2005 to his eight-month pregnant neighbour who was carrying another man's child.

220. Toilet Day: PMO to Home, rank decides where you go

New Delhi: The country may have more mobile phones than toilets but answering the call of nature, it seems, is determined by the pecking order even in some top government offices in the nation's capital which do not have a dearth of rest rooms. The affirmative action apparently aims to allow senior officers to ease themselves in cleaner facilities and is in practice in no less than the Prime Minister's Office, the Home Ministry, Environment Ministry, the Department of personnel and Training and the Directorate General of Civil Aviation, to name a few.

The PMO, in fact, issued a circular as recently as August 23, 2013 to remind those working there about where they could go or not go. "It has been observed that staff not entitled to use

If people can laugh more, the world will certainly be better. And if people can laugh in situations when laughter does not come easily, the world can become tremendously different, a very happy world.

these toilets is using the same, leaving the premises dirty," the circular said referring to toilets reserved for senior officers. "To avoid any embarrassing situation, all staff members are expected to refrain from using toilets that are exclusively marked **'For Officers Only'**, failing which administration will be constrained to take suitable action against staff defaulting on this count."

221. Only 20K Parsis in India by next century

Mumbai: The number of Parsis worldwide is dropping by the day, and India accounts for a chunk of it. Going by the current birth rate of the community by the next century, there will be less than 20,000 Parsis in India. For any population to remain stable, the fertility rate – the average number of children per woman – should be 2.1. But the community's fertility rate standing at 0.89, solutions are needed urgently, agrred the members.

A 45-minute - long session on 'Late marriages and divorce amongst Parsis', which focused on declining count of Parsis due to no or late marriage and high rate of divorce with mutual consent has increased. Girls are not interested in marrying early and if they do, they marry outside their community. It was suggested that ***'Jiyo Parsi'*** scheme should be launched by the government to curb the population decline.

222. IRS Officer booked for video on wife

Nagpur: An IRS Officer has been booked for allegedly making an obscene video of his wife and using it to blackmail her for dowry. Bangalore resident Nishwant Davrajan Kullulathil was booked on Wednesday (19th September, 2012 along with his mother and sister under Sections of the Domestic Violence, Sexual

In my mind, there is nothing so illiberal and so ill-bred as audible laughter.

Offence and Dowry Prohibition Act. Nishant's wife, an assistant income tax officer, lodged a complaint with police against her husband for sodomising her in Nagpur, and threatening her with her videos if she did not give him ₹10 lakh.

223. 'My brother was over 100 kg, he was killed over 250 gm of jalebis'

New Delhi: A delay in serving a customer jalebis cost Satender Singh (30), a salesman at Bangla Sweet House in Gole-Market, his life. He was shot in the head by the security guard, Neeraj Kumar, who works with CMS security Solutions Company. The man, seemed to be drunk, came and asked for 250 gms of jalebis. Satender was frying the jalebis, asked him to stand in queue. He went away and returned with pistol and pulled the trigger at Satender's temple. Satender's brother Sonu Singh said "My brother weighed over 100 kg. He was killed for 250 gms of jalebis."

224. Eldest leaves the House of Elders

New Delhi: A little after 5 pm on Wednesday (19th February, 2014), as the Rajya Sabha adjourned for the day, Shri Rishang Keishing, 94-year-old (born on 25th October, 1920), at present, Member of Parliament (Rajya Sabha) from Manipur, quietly left his seat and headed for exit – for the last time in his life. Shri Rishang, MP since 1952 is **the oldest serving parliamentarian in the world.** His term in the upper house ends on April 9, 2014. No one saw him off; no TV cameras followed him, as Keishing, unescorted and unnoticed, hailed his car to leave the Parliament complex. He said he liked it this way. "I have had enough. I'm glad to go."

It's hard to be funny when you have to be clean.

225. Difference in breast milk for male and female babies

London: A mother's milk may contain different levels of nutrients depending on the sex of her baby to meet different growth needs. Scientists believe that mothers make breast milk differently for male and female babies.

226. Femen calls for 'topless jihad'

Washington: Infamous Ukrainian feminists group Femen has declared April 4 as Topless Jihad Day in support of a Tunisian activist, 19, who was threatened to death by stoning after she posted two topless pictures online. The Femen group said "long live the topless jihad against infidels! Our tits are deadlier than your stones!" Countless women have posted photos on the Femen Facebook page in solidarity of Amina Tyler. Femen also called on women to bare their breasts as a show of solidarity after which true freedom, freedom without mullahs and caliphs, will come to Tunisia.

227. Good News: In MP village, bride gives birth to baby at wedding mandap

Bhopal: In Dindori district's Bichchia village, 466 km. from Bhopal, a bride gave birth to a baby at her own wedding mandap. Damyanti Bai and the groom, Ram Singh, were in the middle of the ritual pheras round the fire, when Damyanti went into labour. Shocked relatives from both families as well as community members wanted to call off the wedding, but the groom would not hear of it. Singh requested guests to stay on despite warnings from the elders of the community, who threatened to penalise him if married Damyanti. He said any penalty as decided by the community panchayat but could

---

Laughter does not seem to be a sin, but it leads to sin.

---

not abandon his bride. "The day I was engaged to her, I had promised to support her throughout life."

228. Telephone woes plague Prez home

Bolpur: When it comes to telephone snags, even the head of the state can't hope for any respite. The landline registered in the name of President Pranab Mukherjee at his ancestral home at Kirnahar, Birbhum goes dead regularly – about three to four times a month – and it has been plaguing his family members for years. The connection was installed in 1967 when Mukherjee became a Rajya Sabha member for the first time. "I am old and I am comfortable only with the landline. Whenever this phone is dead, which is often, I can't speak to any relative or friends," Annapurna Banerjee, sister of Pranab Mukherjee.

229. Chennai woman lawyer to wed life convict

Chennai: The story of a woman advocate marrying a life convict, who is in jail for 12 years in a murder case, may seem straight out of a film. But Chennai will witness one such marriage on February 2, when 27-year-old advocate. A. Aruna marries 38-year-old Somasundaram, alias Somu, at a village hall in Vyasarpadi. The bride herself filed a petition in the Madras High Court, seeking 30 days' special leave from prison for her groom. A division bench, comprising Justice S. Rajeswaran and Justice P.N. Prakash, passing order on Bhuvna's habeas corpus plea, granted Somu 10 days' leave.

230. A kiss gives away French jewel thief

London: A jewel thief in France who kissed the owner of a jewellery shop during a robbery was nabbed after police analysed the DNA on the victim's cheek. The robber had kissed the 58-year-old woman apologetically after gagging her for hours. A forensic team swabbed her cheek and the man's DNA was found in the national genetic print database. He was traced to a jail.

231. Principal makes 11-year-old drink urine in Gujarat

Ahmedabad: A Class 6 student of Don Bosco English School at Vejapur was allegedly forced to drink his urine by the principal after the student was found urinating in a plastic bottle in a empty classroom. He was then taken by a peon to the primary school principal. The student said that after the fourth period, he had gone down to the ground floor but there was a long queue at the urinal. "I also noticed that I had left behind my snack-box in my classroom, I rushed back to my classroom where there is no urinal and I felt an urgent need to pie."

232. Cell phone saves man from tigress

Jabalpur: The 50-something resident of the Adivasi-dominated Baihar village (heavily tiger-infested territory, barely 10 km. off the Kanha national park) in Balaghat district recently had a close encounter with death. Dairy owner Beniram Rangdale spent an agonizing three hours up on a tree with a furious tigress waiting below, just when he thought it was all over, his mobile phone came to rescue. He sent out a telephonic SOS to his friends and the search party that arrived soon managed to secure the tigress away. Five days later, the handset has joined the resident deities who sit in the 'puja' alcove of the Rangdale household. He will not part with his lucky phone at any price. In the instant case, God took the form of a mobile phone.

233. UK girl, 9, reads 364 books in seven months

London: A nine-year-old, Faith of Ashley, Cheshire, voracious reader in the UK has managed to read an incredible 364 books in just seven months. She shuns the television and computer games, and prefers to settle down with either Roald Dahl or a Harry Potter book.

234. Dream come true: ATM in MP dispenses double cash

Bhopal: State Bank of India officials went into a tizzy after one of its ATMs in Madhya Pradesh's Mansa town began spewing extra cash, nearly double the amount keyed in by customers. As words spread, crowds thronged the kiosk to collect their booty. For a withdrawal request of [1] 5,000 the machine was ejecting [1] 10,000. The free-for-all that started in the morning continued till 10 pm., when SBI officials finally got a wind of its depleting coffers and sent an SOS to police to shut down the ATM. Cops swiftly cleared the crowd, but nearly [1] 4.5 lakh extra had been withdrawn by then. [1] 8 lakh was still left. [1] 2.5 lakh was recovered. Thousand-rupee-notes were stashed in trays marked for [1] 500 rupee-notes inside the machine. However, the slips delivered against transactions did not bill the extra amount delivered by the ATM.

235. Maths no bar

Jagraon: Politicians can go to any length to please their leaders – even arithmetic fails prey to it. Sample this: When Punjab chief minister Prakash Singh Badal went to Jagraon to take stock of preparations for Narendra Modi's rally, he asked local MLA S.R. Kler about the number of people he would bring from his constituency. Kler said 20,000, prompting a question about transport arrangements. Twenty buses have been arranged, the MLA replied promptly. ***"Tissi ik bus wich kinne bande bithaoge... hisaab taan theek theek laga to (How many people would you carry in one bus. Check your maths),"*** retorted the CM, leaving the poor legislator scratching his head.

236. Babas, tantriks prey on Indians in United Kingdom

London: Old and new migrants from India are among the most successful in the UK. But scratch the glittering surface and the reality is that a large section of community sustain a 40 million pound 'industry' of babas and tantriks who promise to deliver love, luck and lure for a price. Pick up any newspaper published here in Indian or Asian languages, or switch on any 'ethnic' television channel, and chances are you will be greeted by adverts on 'babas', mystics and astrologers, promising magic cure for ailments and removing bad spells, among other attractions. Many such 'babas' travel here from India and other parts of south Asia for a brief period, offer their 'services' to the superstitious in the community for a fee, and return home. Most victims do not complain to authorities after realising they have been conned.

237. UN too Christian, claims latest NGO report

United Nations: Christianity dominates the United Nations and more diversity is needed to increase non-Christian representation in world peace-making, according to a study. The research has revealed that more than 70% of religious non-government organisations (NGOs) at the UN are Christian, and that there is historical privilege in allowing the Vatican a special observer status, as both a state and a religion.

238. Man donates organs, saves his father

New Delhi: Few are born with the spirit of Santosh Verma, 35, but it is something worth emulating. In a country where organ donation is still not a common practice, Verma donated two of his organs within a period of two years to save his father's life. He donated half of his liver in April, 2012 when his father C.P. Verma's (63) liver was damaged. A year later, when it was discovered that his father's kidneys had been damaged, he came forward to donate one of his kidneys as there was no other donor in the family. The second transplant was done in December, 2013. "Organ transplant should not be a medical issue, it should be considered a social issue in our country. Both father & son are absolutely fine now.

239. Vigilance complaints pile up as Delhi doesn't know password

New Delhi: Over 600 complaints regarding the Delhi Police forwarded by the Central Vigilance Commission to an online portal have been pending for the past eight years. The reason: the Delhi Police didn't know the password to access the portal or how to operate it, a lapse that went undetected since 2006.

Incidentally, the Delhi Police recently advertised that anyone could now lodge a complaint with it online about a missing object – "A first for the country." Hopefully, with better luck.

240. Laser hair removal goes wrong, a man's arm gets burnt

New Delhi: His marriage proposal turned down because he had too much body hair, a 26-year-old gazetted railway officer approached what he believed was one of the best centres for laser treatment (New Look Cosmetic Skin Laser Centre at Lajpat Nagar). But during the course of treatment to rid his body of excess hair, Himmat Ram Meena's right arm got burnt.

241. From betting to murder, Ujjain resident a witness in 300 cases

Bhopal: Pankaj Sanchora, 43, is a newspaper vendor and a part-time property agent. He is also almost a full-time prosecution witness, having been named as a witness in not less than 300 criminal cases, according to available records.

From relatively minor crimes like gambling and betting to more serious offences like looting, chain-snatching and even rapes and murders, the Ujjain resident is reported to have deposed in about 240 cases in the last 23 years, with trials in at least another 60 cases still pending. The police admitted they make him a witness because he is readily available.

242. Corporate coaching offered for netas

New Delhi: You have heard of B-schools that turn out business managers. Fancy a P-school that turns out political leaders?

A US-based company, "Leadership Circle," which usually coaches business leaders for giant corporations like Microsoft, thinks India's netas could do with some coaching – and eyes them as a potential market. "It will be hugely successful for politicians, if they are willing to be assessed. Politicians are also human beings," said Pratap Nambiar, director, Leadership Circle's Indian unit.

243. Man killed over ₹300, three arrested

Indore: Three men were arrested on the charge of killing a friend after he refused to pay ₹300 lost over a game of carom, the accused mercilessly beat to death Prakash Suryawanshi alias Munna after he refused to pay the money betted during a carrom game.

244. No to sex during honeymoon is not cruelty: HC

Mumbai: Refusal to have sex with a life partner during honeymoon does not amount to cruelty, the Bombay High Court has ruled while setting aside a family court judgement, dissolving the marriage of a couple on this ground.

245. India 111th among nations with women MPs

United Nations: India is placed at the 111th position out of 189 countries in a list prepared by an international organisation that ranks nation on the number of women representatives in Parliament. India ranked 111th with 62 women Parliamentarians sitting in its Lower House, a small 11.4% of the total 545 MPs. The Upper House of 245 MPs has 28 women Parliamentarians, a 11.4% of the total.

246. 5,000-year-old tradition of 'itra' hit by gutkha ban

New Delhi: A 5,000-year-old tradition is suffering a setback as sale of itra or attar, the non-alcoholic fragrance extracted from plant parts, has gone down-hill, interestingly, due to a ban on tobacco products.

"The tobacco industry accounts for about 50-60% of the demand for itra as flavour. Hence the gutkha ban has led to a nearly 50% decline in sale of the naturally derived products."

Prayer is a play. So if you go to the temple and you become very serious. Go to the temple of laugh, go to the temple of enjoy.

---

247. End of the road for 50p coins

Mumbai: The humble 50 paise coins is still legal tender, but could be close to extinction given that people refuse to accept it.

From shopkeepers to traders, laundrymen, rickshaw drivers, bus commuters and provision store owners, the smallest denomination of the Indian currency is simply not acceptable anymore. Although it is illegal to decline a coin still in circulation, the public seem to have made up it mind. The raging inflation has made it virtually worthless.

248. Dalit teen can't pay to cheat in exam, immolates himself

Lucknow: A Class 10 Dalit student (17-year-old Akash), who had set himself on fire after being unable to write his board exams as he could not pay the amount (₹4,000) allegedly demanded by his school principal to allow him to copy and cheat, died of burn injuries.

249. Chocolate main offering in Kerala temple

Alappuzha (Kerala): If you are planning a visit to the Thekkan Palani temple in Kerala make sure you take a few chocolate bars with you to offer the presiding deity.

The traditional offerings of oil, flowers, coconut or incense sticks just won't do as the temple is home to Balamurugan – Lord Muruga, son of Lord Shiva, as a child. In fact the offering of a particular brand of chocolate has become so pervasive that the deity has been nicknamed 'Munch Murugan'. Even the 'prasadam' given to the devotees includes a portion of the bar along with flowers and sandal paste.

Remember one thing: it is only man who can cry and laugh.

250. 'Offensive' letter in bag claims girl's life

Guwahati: A 12-year-old girl committed suicide by immolating herself after a teacher allegedly punished her for carrying an 'objectionable letter' in her schoolbag.

The girl, Nibedita Dey, was a class 5 student of the English medium Sophy Mercy School in eastern Assam's Sivasagar town, some 400 km. from Guwahati. She was the daughter of a college lecturer. The girl's ordeal began after the school authorities found the letter and told her to inform her parents for a meeting. She did not, fearing punishment from her parents.

The Principal, a woman, allegedly tortured Nibedita mentally and physically in school the next day. On Saturday (8th March, 2014), she set herself on fire when no one was around. She succumbed to burn injuries on Sunday. In a statement in the hospital, Nibedita said she was innocent and was framed.

251. Khan's buffaloes home cops get transfer orders

Lucknow/Meerut: Though all seven stolen buffaloes (seven sisters) of urban development minister Azam Khan were recovered. Ekta Tirha police station in-charge, sub-inspector Sunil Kumar, and constables Ajay and Bipin have been sent to the police lines. The police station covers the Mandakini chowk area where the minister's cattle house is located. The massive hunt, led by SSP Sadhna Goswami, for the minister's buffaloes - complete with sniffer dog.

Enigma of return: Slowly, inexorably, buffaloes always come home.

It is almost politically incorrect to speak of India's cow belt these days but after the absurd police dragnet laid out for Samajwadi Party leader Azam Khan's barnyard assets in Rampur, "buffalo belt" may gain traction. India's most placid and tractable mammal has effortlessly exercised the imagination, the government, the police, the media, everything and everybody except Azam Khan himself, who has drily thanked the press for the free publicity. A buffalo hunt was unleashed; their retreating hoof prints were sniffed by police dogs. The media treated them as a huge black joke. No quite, three policemen were suspended in UP, collateral damage of the buffalo hunt.

WORDLY WISE: Ellsworth Huntington - The buffalo is a surprisingly stupid animal.

UNQUOTE: Someone believes Khan's buffaloes might have gone on 5-Village Study Tour, if not a case of abduction, political move or "Love-affairs."

***Chalte Chalte*:** "My buffaloes more famous than Queen Victoria. Switch on the television and you find *bhaisein aagey-aagey, aur main peechhe-peechhe, aur sir pe gobar" : Azam*
Bhag Bhains Bhag.

Reference

UNIQUE News has been compiled from Hindustan Times (HT), Patna, Times of India (TOI), Patna, The Indian Express (IE), New Delhi, The Hindu, Chennai.

1. 25.3.2010 (TOI)
2. 25.8.2012 (IE)
3. 11.7.2011 (IE)
4. 12.11.2011 (TOI)
5. 13.2.2012 (HT)
6. 25.3.2012 (IE)
7. 25.3.2012 (HT)
8. 29.4. 2012 (TOI)
9. 9.5.2012 (HT)
10. 23.5.2012 (HT)
11. 1.9.2012 (TOI)
12. 21.9.2012 (HT)
13. 23.9.2012 (HT)
14. 1.11.2013 (HT)
15. 6.10.2012 (IE)
16. 7.10.2012 (HT)
17. 5.11.2012 (IE)
18. 9.12.2012 (IE)
19. 29.12.2012 (TOI)
20. 12.12.2012 (HT)
21. 15.12.2012 (HT)
22. 25.12.2012 (HT)
23. 29.12.2012 (Hindu)
24. 3.1.2013 (HT)
25. 4.1.2013 (Hindu)
26. 10.1.2013 (HT)
27. 23.1.2013 (Hindu)
28. 3.2.2013 (TOI)
29. 20.2.2013 (HT)
30. 19.2.2013 (IE)
31. 21.2.2013 (HT)
32. 23.2.2013 (IE)
33. 25.2.2013 (HT)
34. 26.2.2013 (IE)
35. 25.2.2013 (HT)
36. 3.3.2013 (IE)
37. 4.3.2013 (IE)
38. 17.3.2013 (HT)
39. 17.3.2013 (HT)
40. 18.3.2013 (HT)
41. 19.3.2013 (IE)
42. 24.3.2013 (TOI)
43. 31.3.2013 (HT)
44. 15.4.2013 (HT)
45. 15.4.2013 (HT)
46. 19.4.2013 (HT)
47. 19.4.2013 (HT)
48. 20.4.2013 (HT)
49. 21.4.2013 (HT)
50. 25.4.2013 (HT)
51. 2.5.2013 (IE)
52. 4.5.2013 (IE)
53. 5.5.2013 (IE)
54. 9.5.2013 (IE)
55. 18.5.2013 (HT)
56. 19.5.2013 (IE)
57. 27.5.2013 (HT)
58. 31.5.2013 (IE)
59. 4.6.2013 (IE)
60. 11.6.2013 (IE)
61. 11.6.2013 (IE)
62. 16.6.2013 (IE)
63. 24.6.2013 (IE)
64. 28.6.2013 (HT)
65. 14.7.2013 (IE)
66. 4.7.2013 (IE)
67. 4.7.2013 (HT)
68. 23.7.2013 (HT)
69. 25.7.2013 (IE)
70. 29.7.2013 (HT)
71. 10.8.2013 (HT)
72. 10.8.20132 (HT)
73. 11.8.2013 (TOI)
74. 11.8.2013 (HT)
75. 12.8.2013 (IE)
76. 16.8.2013 (IE)
77. 20.8.2013 (HT)
78. 21.8.2013 (HT)
79. 21.8.2013 (IE)
80. 27.8.2013 (HT)
81. 11.7.2011 (IE)
82. 28.8.2013 (HT)
83. 29.8.2013 (HT)
84. 29.8.2013 (IE)
85. 2.9.2013 (TOI)
86. 4.9.2013 (HT)
87. 6.9.2013 (HT)
88. 9.9.2013 (HT)
89. 9.9.2013 (HT)
90. 10.9.2013 (IE)
91. 12.9.2013 (HT)
92. 13.9.2013 (HT)
93. 13.9.2013 (IE)
94. 14.9.2013 (IE)
95. 15.9.2013 (HT)
96. 18.9.2013 (Hindu)
97. 19.9.2013 (IE)
98. 19.9.2013 (IE)
99. 20.9.2013 (HT)
100. 21.9.2013 (IE)
101. 24.9.2013 (HT)
102. 25.9.2013 (HT)
103. 27.9.2013 (HT)
104. 29.9.2013 (HT)
105. 10.10.2013 (HT)
106. 10.10.2013 (HT)
107. 16.10.2013 (IE))
108. 10.10.2013 (IE)
109. 16.10.2013 (HT)
110. 17.10.2013 (HT)
111. 18.10.2013 (HT)
112. 15.10.2013 (HT)
113. 19.10.2013 (IE)
114. 22.10.2013 (IE)
115. 24.10.2013 (IE)
116. 25.10.2013 (IE)
117. 28.10.2013 (HT)

Laughter is dead when vacancy in the head.
***With humour, there is life** – JR.*

118. 28.10.2013 (HT)
119. 29.10.2013 (HT)
120. 6.11.2013 (HT)
121. 6.11.2013 (IE)
122. 31.1.2014 (HT)
123. 8.11.2013 (HT)
124. 6.11.2013 (IE)
125. 10.11.2013 (HT)
126. 10.11.2013 (HT)
127. 7.9.2013 (HT)
128. 12.11.2013 (IE)
129. 13.11.2013 (HT)
130. 18.11.2013 (HT)
131. 18.11.2013 (HT)
132. 21.11.2013 (HT)
133. 21.11.2013 (IE)
134. 22.11.2013 (IE)
135. 28.11.2013 (IE)
136. 1.12.2013 (HT)
137. 1.12.2013 (HT)
138. 2.12.2013 (IE)
139. 2.12.2013 (IE)
140. 6.12.2013 (Hindu)
141. 7.12.2013 (HT)
142. 8.12.2013 (Hindu)
143. 8.12.2013 (TOI)
144. 10.12.2013 (TOI)
145. 12.12.2013 (TOI)
146. 13.12.2013 (HT)
147. 13.12.2013 (HT)
148. 132.12.2013 (IE)
149. 13.12.2013 (IE)
150. 13.12.2013 (IE)
151. 16.12.2013 (HT)
152. 13.12.2013 (HT)
153. 17.12.2013 (IE)
154. 17.12.2013 (IE)
155. 19.12.2013 (HT)
156. 19.12.2013 (IE)
157. 20.12.2013 (HT)
158. 21.12.2013 (HT)
159. 22.12.2013 (IE)
160. 23.12.2013 (IE)
161. 26.12.2013 (HT)
162. 31.12.2013 (HT)
163. 4.2.2014 (HT)
164. 31.12.2013 (IE)
165. 31.12.20'13 (IE)
166. 31.12.2013 (IE)
167. 15.9.2013 (HT)
168. 15.9.2013 (HT)
169. 1.1.2014 (HT)
170. 1.1.2014 (IE)
171. 2.1.2014 (HT)
172. 2.1.2014 HT)
173. 3.1.2014 (HT)
174. 5.1.2014 (HT)
175. 5.1.2014 HT)
176. 6.1.2014 (HT)
177. 6.1.2014 (IE)
178. 6.1.2014 (IE)
179. 7.1.2014 (IE)
180. 9.1.2014 (HT)
181. 10.1.2014 (HT)
182. 10.1.2014 (HT)
183. 13.1.2014 (HT)
184. 15.1.2014 (HT)
185. 16.1.2014 (IE)
186. 17.1.2014 (IE)
187. 18.1.2014 (HT)
188. 19.1.2014 (IE)
189. 20.1.2014 (HT)
190. 21.1.2014 (HT)
191. 23.1.2014 (IE)
192. 23.1.2014 (IE)
193. 25.1.2014 (Hindu)
194. 26.1.2014 (HT)
195. 27.1.2014 (IE)
196. 27.1.2014 (IE)
197. 24.12.2013 (TOI)
198. 6.1.2014 (TOI)
199. 112.3.2011(HT)
200. 30.3.2011(HT)
201. 1.4.2011 (HT)
202. 20.5.2011 (IE)
203. 8.2.2014 (IE)
204. 8.2.2014 (IE)
205. 9.2.2014 (HT)
206. 23.2.2014 (IE)
207. 24.2.2014 (IE)
208. 18.1.2014 (IE)
209. 6.2.2014 (HT)
210. 5.2.2014 (IE)
211. 14.9.2013 (TOI)
212. 26.12.2013 (TOI)
213. 26.12.2013 (TOI)
214. 13.9.2013 (TOI)
215. 11.9.2013 (TOI)
216. 5.10.2013 (TOI)
217. 30.8.2013 (TOI)
218. 11.9.2.2014 (IE)
219. 2.11.2013 (TOI)
220. 22.11.2013 (IE)
221. 29.12.2013 (IE)
222. 21.09.2012 (HT)
223. 20.02.2014 (IE)
224. 20.02.2014 (IE)
225. 18.02.214 (HT)
226. 03.03.2013 (HT)
227. 23.02.2014 (HT)
228. 23.02.2014 (HT)
229. 02.02.2014 (TOI)
230. 06.02.2014 (TOI)
231. 10.02.2014 (TOI)
232. 12.12.2014 (TOI)
233. 17.02.2014 (TOI)
234. 21.02.2014 (TOI)
235. 26.02.2014 (HT)
236. 09.01.2014 (HT)
237. 02.01.2014 (HT)
238. 15.01.2014 (HT)
239. 3.3.2014 (IE)
240. 5.3.2014 (IE)
241. 7.3.2014 (IE)
242. 9.3.2014 (HT)
243. 9.3.2014 (HT)
244. 10.3.2014 (HT)
245. 9.3.2014 (HT)
246. 4.3.2014 (TOI)
247. 11.3.2014 (TOI)
248. 11.3.2014 (IE)
249. 12.3.2014 (HT)
250. 11.3.2014 (HT)
251. 4.2.2014 (IE)

Laughter is God's blessings – *Joseph Prince.*
Laughter is inner jogging – *Norman Cousins.*
